Cymbeline

by William Hawkins

1759

A FACSIMILE PUBLISHED BY CORNMARKET PRESS
FROM THE COPY IN THE BIRMINGHAM SHAKESPEARE LIBRARY
LONDON
1969

PUBLISHED BY CORNMARKET PRESS LIMITED
42/43 CONDUIT STREET LONDON W1R ONL
PRINTED IN ENGLAND BY FLETCHER AND SON LIMITED NORWICH

SBN 7191 0119 0

CYMBELINE.

A TRAGEDY,

ALTERED FROM

SHAKESPEARE.

As it is perform'd at the

THEATRE-ROYAL in Covent-Garden.

By WILLIAM HAWKINS, M.A.
Late Fellow of Pembroke College, and Professor of
Poetry in the University of Oxford.

LONDON:
Printed for JAMES RIVINGTON and JAMES FLETCHER,
at the Oxford Theatre, in Pater-noster-row. MDCCLIX.

[Price One Shilling and Six-pence.]

1759.

PR
2878
.C7
H3
1969

TO THE

RIGHT HONOURABLE THE

Countess of Litchfield.

MADAM,

I Have the honour of your LADY-SHIP's permission to present to you a Tragedy, which, though it met with numerous and unprecedented difficulties and discouragements in the theatre, will, I hope, be thought not altogether unworthy your protection in the world.—Indeed, if the unpopularity of its late situation could in the least affect that degree of merit, which your LADYSHIP's candor, or the indulgence of the town, may allow it to have, it would ill become me to recommend it to my readers, under the sanction of so polite and illustrious a name.—But your LADYSHIP has too much good sense, as well as generosity, to judge of this performance by mere appearances, and accidental or unlucky circumstances; and therefore, tho' it will stand as a kind of memorial of the bad fortune, and worse treatment of its author; it may at the same time be a proper testimony of the high respect with which I am,

Madam,

Your Ladyship's

most obliged

Feb. 22, 1759.

and most obedient Servant,

WILLIAM HAWKINS.

PREFACE.

THE Tragedy of *Cymbeline* is, in the whole oeconomy of it, one of the most irregular productions of *Shakespeare*. Its defects however, or rather its superfluities, are more than equalled by beauties, and excellencies of various kinds. There is at the same time something so pleasingly romantic, and likewise truly *British* in the subject of it, that, I flatter myself, an attempt to reduce it, as near as possible, to the regular standard of the *drama*, will be favourably received by all, who are admirers of *novelty*, when *propriety* is its foundation. I have accordingly endeavoured to new-construct this Tragedy, almost upon the plan of *Aristotle* himself, in respect of the *unity* of *Time*; with so thorough a veneration however for the great *Father* of the *English* stage, that, even while I have presumed to regulate and modernize his design, I have thought it an honour to tread in his steps, and to imitate his Stile, with the humility and reverence of a *Son*. With this view, I have retained in *many* places the very language of the original author, and in *all* others endeavoured to supply it with a diction similar thereunto; so that, as an unknown friend of mine has observed, the present attempt is intirely *new*, whether it be considered as an *alteration from*, or an *imitation of Shakespeare*.

—The *difficulty* of such an attempt, as *rational* as it may be, has a kind of *claim*, I presume, to the *indulgence* of the public; especially as it has been attended likewise with *disadvantages*.—For I found myself necessitated by my plan to *drop some* characters, to *contract others*, and to omit *some* scenes and incidents of an interesting nature;—or rather to bring the substance and purport of them within the compass of a few short narrations.—A loss irreparable this, but that conveniencies are likewise to be thrown into the opposite scale; for as, I hope, I have not *injured* any characters by *contracting* them, but have left them to *all intents*, and in point of *importance* the *same*; so I have had an opportunity of *enlarging* and *improving some* of the original parts, (those particularly of *Palador*, and *Philario*, the *Pisanio of Shakespeare*) and, by varying certain incidents and circumstances, of giving a *new cast* to the whole *drama*.—After all, I am very far from meaning to detract from the merit of *Shakespeare*; or from insinuating that the plays of so exalted a genius *require* such

new-

PREFACE.

new-modelling as the present, in order to the rendering them useful or entertaining.—I have ventured publicly to defend this great *dramatic* Poet in the liberties he has taken; but still *Shakespeare* himself needs not be *ashamed* to *wear* a *modern dress*, provided it can be made tolerably to *fit* him.

The only question then will be, whether the present *alteration* be a judicious one?——And this with all due deference is left to the candour and justice of the public.

It will be proper to acquaint the reader, that, this play, was recommended some time since by a person of the first distinction, to the manager of the other theatre; who declared, that he had the very same altered play in his possession, and that it was designed for representation on his stage. Our *Cymbeline* therefore was obliged to take up his head-quarters at *Covent-Garden*; where he has contended not only with the *usual* difficulties, but also with *others* of an *extraordinary* nature——Mrs. *Bellamy*'s declining the part of *Imogen* has done the play incredible prejudice; and convinces me of the vanity of striving against the stream of popularity in general, or the weight of particular disadvantages. ——However, I am under obligations to *many of* of the performers, for their best endeavours to do justice to my piece, and for their zeal for its success. To *some* I am indebted for real service, whose names, as comparisons are invidious, I leave it to the judgment of the reader to supply.

Upon the whole, I am at a loss to ballance the account between myself and my fortune, in this whimsical situation. The kind assistance, and, I hope, not extremely partial approbation of *some*, adds as much to my *credit* and *satisfaction*, as the *delicacy*, or *ill-nature*, &c. of *others*, has deducted from my *advantages*.———To my *friends*, I return my sincere acknowledgments, and best wishes; to my *enemies*, I shall say nothing, 'till they are *candid*, and *sagacious* enough to speak more *plainly* than they have hitherto done,——and more *to the purpose*.

PROLOGUE.

Spoken by Mr. Ross.

BRITONS, the daring Author of to-night,
Attempts in Shakespear's manly stile to write;
He strives to copy from that mighty mind
The glowing vein — the spirit unconfin'd —
The figur'd diction that disdain'd controul ——
And the full vigour of the poet's soul!
—Happy the varied phrase, if none shall call,
This imitation, that original.——

For other points, our new advent'rer tries
The bard's luxuriant plan to modernize;
And, by the rules of antient art, refine
The same eventful, pleasing, bold design.

Our scenes awake not now the am'rous flame,
Nor teach soft swains to woo the tender dame;
Content, for bright example's sake, to shew
A wife distress'd, and innocence in woe.—
For what remains, the poet bids you see,
From an old tale, what Britons ought to be;
And in these restless days of war's alarms,
Not melts the soul to love, but fires the blood to arms.

(x)

Your great forefathers scorn'd the foreign chain,
Rome might invade, and Cæsars rage in vain —
Those glorious patterns with bold hearts pursue,
To king, to country, and to honour true! —

Oh! then with candour and good will attend,
Applaud the author in the cordial friend:
Remember, when his failings most appear,
It ill becomes the brave to be severe. —
Look ages back, and think you hear to-night
An antient poet, still your chief delight!
Due to a great attempt compassion take,
And spare the modern bard for Shakespear's sake.

EPILOGUE

Spoken by Mrs. VINCENT.

WELL, Sirs — the bus'ness of the day is o'er,
And I'm a princess, and a wife no more —
This bard of our's, with Shakespear in his head,
May be well-taught, but surely is ill-bred.
Spouse gone, coast clear, wife handsome, and what not,
We might have had a much genteeler plot.
What madness equals true poetic rage?
Fine stuff! a lady in a hermitage!
A pretty mansion for the blooming fair ——
No tea, no scandal, — no intriguing there. ——
———The

—The gay beau-monde such hideous scenes must damn—
What! nothing modish, but one cordial dram!
—Yet after all, the poet bids me say,
For your own credit's sake approve the play;
You can't for shame condemn old British wit,
(I hope there are no Frenchmen in the pit)
Or slight a timely tale, that well discovers,
The bravest soldiers are the truest lovers.

Such Leonatus was, in our romance,
A gallant courtier, tho' he cou'd not dance;
Say, wou'd you gain, like him, the fair one's charms,
First try your might in hardy deeds of arms;
Your muffs, your coffee, and down-beds fore-go,
Follow the mighty Prussia thro' the snow;
At length bring home the honourable scar,
And love's sweet balm shall heal the wounds of war.

For me, what various thoughts my mind perplex?
Is't better I resume my feeble sex,
Or wear this manly garb? it fits me well—
Gallants instruct me—ladies, can you tell?
The court's divided, and the gentle beaux,
Cry—no disguises—give the girl her cloaths.
The ladies say, to-night's example teaches,
(And I will take their words without more speeches)
That things go best when—women wear the breeches.

Dramatis

Dramatis Personæ.

CYMBELINE,	Mr. RYAN.
CLOTEN,	Mr. CLARKE.
LEONATUS,	Mr. ROSS.
PALADOR,	Mr. SMITH.
CADWAL,	Mr. LOWE.
BELLARIUS,	Mr. SPARKES.
PHILARIO,	Mr. RIDOUT.
C. LUCIUS,	Mr. GIBSON.
PISANIO,	Mr. DYER.
TWO LORDS.	
IMOGEN,	Mrs. VINCENT.

OFFICERS, SOLDIERS, &c.

SCENE, partly a Royal Castle, and partly in and near a Forest in WALES.

CYMBELINE.

A

TRAGEDY.

ACT I.

SCENE *A Royal Palace.*

Enter two LORDS.

1st LORD.

Pray you feaſt mine ears with more of this;
For 'tis ſo long ſince firſt I turn'd my back
Upon our iſle, that I am new in Britain.

2d LORD.

I think your wiſh to breathe in foreign air,
Took you away about the very time
The royal babes were ſtolen.

1st LORD.

It is true, ſir—
Some twenty years ago — 'twas a ſtrange theft,

B But

But the concealment stranger; for you tell me,
That to this hour there is no guess in knowlege
Which way they went.

2d LORD.

Was hot in the enquiry — but much time
Has worn out all that miracle — fresh matter
Supplying wonder since.

1st LORD.

     Of which my ignorance
Is not yet perfect learner.

2d LORD.

     Well then, heed me.
Our late good queen (you knew her, sir) whose age
Was thought t'advance beyond more hope of children,
Yet brought the joyful Cymbeline a daughter,
And to his kingdoms a most hopeful heir,
In lieu of those he lost: for Imogen
(Such is her name) took all the graces in,
Which the best wisdom of the times put to her,
As we do air, fast as 'tis minister'd.
If beauty, innocence, and gentleness
Are woman's rarest jewels, she is rich
In most full measure of possession.

1st LORD.

You speak her fair.

2d LORD.

     But not to flatter, sir,
Tho' I should talk the sun down. You have heard

CYMBELINE.

The bright fide of the ftory, for the other
It has a fable hue — I'll be brief with it ——

1ft LORD.
Do, but be plain.

2d LORD.
    The queen quits mortal being;
And Cymbeline, tho' now in wane of life,
Takes to his lonely bed a fecond dame,
A widow, bold, ambitious, cunning, cruel,
That rul'd his heart by acting what fhe was not:
She mov'd the cred'lous king to wed his daughter
With Cloten, her own fon, a wretch in whom
All qualities that dub a worthy man
Are low as worft report. — The princefs caft
Difdain upon his fuit —— and in mean time
My plotting ftepdame dies.

1ft LORD.
     A lucky death!

2d LORD.
'Twas thought fo. —— But the king, in whom this
  weaknefs
Is his firft point of fault, purfues the aim
Of his now dead belov'd, and wills the maid
To take the crown with this encumbrance Cloten,
Or hold her birth-right void.

1ft LORD.
     Alas! poor lady.

2d LORD.
Nay there's more woe behind. — Sweet Imogen
Had long been lift'ning to the earneft fuit
Of Leonatus, a young lord o'th' court,

A valiant, frank, and honeſt gentleman,
That has no vice, if poverty be none;
And to ſay all, as much unlike to Cloten
As man can be to man.——Him in pure love,
And to undo all aims, ſhe weds, and makes
The deed ſoon known her boaſt: th'enraged king
Sends Leonatus into baniſhment,
And her within the circle of this caſtle
Enforceth to abide, till ſhe conſent
To break her bond to her new-wedded lord
By ſtrong propos'd divorce.——This is the ſum
Of what you wiſh'd to hear.

1ſt LORD.
What ſay the Britons
To theſe proceedings?

2d LORD.
As their humours vary;
Some blame the king, all pity Imogen,
And much lament the loſs of Leonatus,
Now the black Romans ſwarm upon our coaſts,
And virtue's call'd to proof.

1ſt LORD.
They're landed then!

2d LORD.
Report ſays loudly ſo.—But hiſt!—the king—
We muſt forbear, we ſhall hear more of this.

Enter CYMBELINE, CLOTEN, *and* Lords.

CYMBELINE,
Well, ſirs, the news abroad?

1ſt LORD.

1st LORD.
So please your majesty,
The Roman legions, all from Gallia drawn,
Are landed on your coast, with large supply
Of Roman gentry, by the senate sent.
CYMBELINE.
Where hold they rendezvous?
2d LORD.
My liege, at Milford.
CYMBELINE.
Now by the soul of great Cassibelan,
They're fairly welcome! — Our right valiant Britons
Will greet them soldier-like.—Cæsar's ambition,
Which swell'd so much that it did almost stretch
The sides o'th' globe, against all colour here
Did put the yoke upon's — which to shake off
Becomes a warlike people, such as we
Will prove ourselves to be.
CLOTEN.
My royal father,
The dreaded foe we have to cope withal
(That in his empire's paw would gripe the world)
Oft have we measur'd swords with — ere't be long
We'll make the mighty name of Cymbeline
To sound as roughly in a Roman ear,
As did Cassibelan's. —
3d LORD.
My gracious liege,
Old Caius Lucius, and th'Italian spark
Pisanio, that was tendant at his side

In

In his late miffion from the Roman camp,
Are come, with errand of efpecial weight
Upon their brow.
CYMBELINE.
   Let them approach our prefence.

Enter C. Lucius, Pisanio, &c.

Lucius, we love thy perfon, tho' thou com'ft
On deputation from our angry foe.
Pifanio, welcome too. Now, firs, the meffage.
LUCIUS.
Firft for myfelf, I thank you, royal fir,
For courtefies receiv'd — not fince forgot ———
My prefent bus'nefs is, in Cæfar's name,
(Cæfar, that hath more kings his fervants than
Thyfelf domeftic officers) to know
If in repentant yielding thou wilt pay
The yearly tribute of three thoufand crowns,
Granted by fam'd Caffibelan thine uncle,
For him and his fucceffion, to great Julius,
(Which by thee lately is untendered left)
Now fell confufion fets his ftandard up,
And fearful wars point at you ?
CYMBELINE.
     Noble Lucius,
Words have no terrors — there be many Cæfars
Ere fuch another Julius ———You well know,
Till the injurious Roman did extort
This tribute, we were free.——— Our Britain is
A world itfelf, and we will nothing pay

         For

CYMBELINE.

For wearing our own faces.— Sir, our subjects
Will not endure this yoke —— and for ourself,
To shew less sov'reignty than they, must needs
Appear unking-like.

LUCIUS.

     Sir, when late to Britain
I came in peaceful embassy to claim
This yet contested tribute, I remember
The boast that fill'd your mouth — you vaunted then
The nat'ral brav'ry of your isle, which stands
As Neptune's park ribbed and paled in
With rocks unscaleable, and roaring waters,
With sands that would not bear your enemies boats,
But suck them up to th' topmast.——We have leaped
This all-forbidding fence,— and, sir, be sure,
Where'er the Roman banner waves in wrath,
Conquest limps not behind.——

[*During this speech*, Cloten *whispers* Pisanio.]

CYMBELINE.

     Had Julius found
In ev'ry land he mangled with his sword,
No stabler footing than he gain'd him here,
I could have bought his empire for a tithe
Of Britain's leanest soil.—— No more of this.
To-morrow we will meet you in the field,
And this fair land is yours, if you can win it;
If not, our crows shall fare the better for you.
         Caius,

Caius, thou'rt welcome: give him tendance, lords,
And feast him as befits his quality;
The due of honour in no point omit.
Once more my hand in friendship; from this time
I wear it as your enemy.

LUCIUS.
     Th' event
Is yet to name the winner. Fare you well.
   [*Exeunt* Lucius, Pisanio, *and some* Lords.

CYMBELINE.
Our expectation that it should be thus
Hath made us forward. Cloten, our now heir,
(For the base Imogen our sometime daughter
Has lost all right in us) *if so it hap*
That I must leave my life in battle, thine
Is this imperial crown.——Great Jupiter
Sprinkle his blessings on't as thou obey'st
Our sov'reign charge.——Hear us most heedily.

CLOTEN.
I do; and will the royal mandate keep
'Mongst my religious bonds.

CYMBELINE.
     Let not our daughter
Breathe more the chearful air of liberty;
This castle be her home, house, region, world,
Till she shall sue thee for the love she scorn'd:
And Leonatus, exil'd, worthless beggar,
That vilely did seduce her young affections,
If with his foot he mark our land again,
      Pursue

Pursue to bitt'rest death.—— So did we promise
Thy mother, our late queen, whose memory yet
Sits fresh upon my heart. Wilt thou do this?

CLOTEN.

My liege, most willingly.

CYMBELINE.

    Then I've laid out
So much of caution well.—— Lords, we must
 bustle ——
It is the common cause that wakes our arms——
We grapple for our own;—— the puny wren
Will chafe him in his thief-assailed nest:
We fight for Britain's franchises, the laws
Of old Mulmutius, our great ancestor,
The first of Britain, which did put his brows
Within a golden crown.

CLOTEN.

    Those laws, great sir,
We will not change for Cæsar's proud behests
That rules by bidding.

CYMBELINE.

    Deal we then our swords
With dextrous resolution; or hereafter
Let them hang up, like utensils discharg'd,
In rusty sloth, and vile disuse for ever.
The gore-besmeared Mars infuse his fury
Into our soldiers breasts; for our own self
We go to battle with a blither heart,
Than ere did jovial bridegroom long repuls'd,
Into his mistress' bed. Sound there aloft

     C   Our

Our inſtruments of war, that Britiſh bloods
May boil to martial muſic.   Forward, paſs.
    [*Flouriſh. Exeunt all but* Cloten.]

Thanks to my mother for this joyleſs crown ——
It fills not half my wiſh: while Leonatus
Reigns in the boſom of fair Imogen,
'Tis I am baniſh'd, and a ſov'reign he:
Wou'd I cou'd pluck their loves up by the roots!
And I am ſtrong in hope —— if young Piſanio
(Whom I made mine by making myſelf Cæſar's
When he was laſt in Britain) hath been true
To the employ I gave him, long ere now
The jealous exile pines him in belief
His lady's truth is tainted.—— Come, Piſanio —
He ſaid, he'd quit the train, and here return
T'unlade his ſecrets to me.— Oh! ſir, welcome!

    Enter PISANIO.

What ſhall I aſk thee firſt? —— How fares Au-
  guſtus?
Is Leonatus mad? Thou might'ſt have told
A hiſtory ere this.
    PISANIO.
     I pray you patience ——
Firſt, ſir, my lord commends him to your high-
  neſs;
Next, the diſeaſed Leonatus hath
Italian fits of jealouſy too ſtrong
For hellebore to cure.

      CLOTEN.

CYMBELINE.

CLOTEN.
That's well —— his grief
Is medicine to mine; but when, and how?
Give me particulars at large —— my ear
Shall catch thy narrative as greedily,
As doth the sick man the kind drops that fall
Upon his fever's flame.

PISANIO.
My lord, as soon
As I had foot in Italy, I challeng'd
Th' abused Leonatus with some friends
To the appointment of a merry meeting;
Where, as the wine danc'd brainward, I began
To praise the freedom of the British ladies,
Their lib'ral hearts, and am'rous 'complishments;
When Leonatus vow'd I did them wrong,
And was too bold in my persuasion.

CLOTEN.
So.

PISANIO.
I fast held me to my sentiment,
And, for his doubt provok'd me, swore myself
Had tasted half the court, and his own princess,
(Whose virtue he had deem'd unparagon'd)
At her own suit in bed.

CLOTEN.
Most brave, brave Roman!

PISANIO.
On this the Briton vaults me from his seat,
And bids my ready sword avow th' affront
Done his pure lady's honour —— I with looks

CYMBELINE

Of calm affurance, and arms folded thus,
Wifh'd him attend my proofs. This fair propofal
Had fanction from all fides, and liquor'd noddles
Joftled to hear my tale.

CLOTEN.
    Why fo —— Proceed.

PISANIO.
Firft, roundly I defcrib'd her bed-chamber,
The arras, cieling, pictures; (for of thefe
I took moft faithful inventory, when
I lay concealed there); then I produc'd
The bracelet that I ravifh'd from her arm,
As fleep, the ape of death, lay dull upon her;
And laft I quoted the cinque-fpotted mole
That richly ftains her breaft, like crimfon drops
I'th'bottom of a cowflip.

CLOTEN.
    There was voucher
Stronger than ever law made.—— Well, fir, what
To this the Briton?

PISANIO.
    He was quite befides
The government of patience —He roll'd round
His bloodfhot eyes, ftamp'd with his foot, and writh'd
His form into all poftures; ftrove to fpeak,
And chatter'd monkey-like;—at length, his choler
Burft into utt'rance rafh —— 'tis well, he cried,
The fiends of hell divide themfelves between
   you ——

         And

CYMBELINE.

And so without more ceremony, left
Our board, to cast conjectures, as they might,
Whereto his fury tended.
CLOTEN.
Thanks, Pisanio;
Saw you him since?
PISANIO.
No; but the rumour was,
Ere I left Rome, that he had turn'd his thought
To bloody purpose of revenge.
CLOTEN.
'Tis good ———
Pisanio, I did love this lady ——— lie
I should not, if I said I love her still ———
O she is sweeter than the breath of spring
Wooing the maiden violet ——— 'tis past ———
And I have lost her.
PISANIO.
She hath wrong'd you.
CLOTEN.
True———
She hath disdain'd me — spurn'd me — once she vow'd,
The meanest garment that e'er clip'd the body
Of Leonatus, was in her respect
Dearer than all the hairs upon my head,
Were they all made such men. ——— The south-fog rot
Him, her, and Cæsar's foes.

PISANIO.

PISANIO.
> Thou wisheft well.—
> This Leonatus is a thorn, my lord,
> That pricks your side of greatnefs. If he 'fcape
> The fnare that traps him now, and haply live
> To recognize his country and his queen,
> Your crown will totter — for the lady keeps
> High feat in ev'ry heart; and for her hufband,
> (I fpeak in envy this) thro' Italy
> Tongues quarrel in his praife; the current voice is,
> So fair an outward, and fuch inward ftuff,
> Endows no man but him.

CLOTEN.
> I prythee ftop —
> Was he not yok'd with Imogen, myfelf
> Could make my tongue a bankrupt in his praife;
> But being what he is, I muft abhor him:
> I have no other hate than what I bear
> Him, and his fortunes; for his kinder ftars
> Have ftill eclipfed mine: but I will fhroud me
> Beneath the Roman wing — Britain, thou haft
> Loud fervice of my tongue; my heart is Cæfar's,
> Of whom I'll hold my crown; thefe reftif Britons
> We muft have curb upon; left gall'd fubjection
> Feeling the heavy lafh of government,
> Fly off from his obedience.

PISANIO.
> Cæfar bad me
> Infure his count'nance, and puiffant arm,
> Who will attack your right —

CLOTEN.

CYMBELINE.   15

CLOTEN.
>   We're bound to him,
Sir, I will post me in th'approaching battle,
Where least our British archers may annoy
The Roman legions.

PISANIO.
>   It is well — but hist —
Who is't comes yonder?

CLOTEN.
>   'Tis Philario, friend
And council-man to Leonatus; best
Abruptly part we here, as chance alone
Had brought us thus together. [*Exeunt severally.*

Enter PHILARIO.

The four-brow'd Cloten!—It is wide suspicion
Thou wear'st cold British heart, and this rencounter
With young Pisanio colours it more strong.
But I have other care.—He writes me here,
>   (*Pulling out letters.*)
In spleenful terms of most confirm'd belief,
That he hath cognizance of her incontinence;
And wills me, by the love and truth I owe him,
To murther her.—Perhaps some false Italian
Hath the infection of foul slander pour'd
In his too ready ear. — Perhaps she's fall'n.—
She's fair,—that's much;—she's young,—that's
>   more, ——— I hold
The virtue of the best attemptable. ———
I must proceed with wary steps herein. —
>   Here's

Here's that will 'tice her from her prison-house,
Or for true love, or seeming.—I will steal
This way to her apartment. [*Exit.*

SCENE *opens, and discovers* Imogen *in her apartment, sitting by a table; a book on the table.*

A father cruel, and a suitor base,
A banish'd husband too — O that's the grief
That gives the deepest wound.—Then am I sure
The shes of Italy will not betray
Mine int'rest, and his honour?— Wicked fear!
Where he abides, falshood is out of fashion,
And truth the law to action.—Hark! the clock!
      (*Clock strikes.*)
'Tis the tenth hour of morn —— the very time
I bad him think on me, and combat heav'n
With prayers, as I would do. —— O bless him
  Gods,
And sweeten all his cares with drops of comfort.
—Now to my book—Philosophy, best doctor,
Thou wisely dost prescribe to human woe
The lenitive of patience. ——   (*Reads.*)

Enter PHILARIO.

     There she sits ——
Sweet student! with a look as chaste as Dian's.—
If she's disloyal, falshood never yet
Hung out so fair a sign—yet *seems*, we know,
Is often read for *is* — I must disturb her ——
Imogen —— lady ——

       IMOGEN.

CYMBELINE.

IMOGEN.
Hah! what now, Philario?
PHILARIO.
Dear lady, here are letters from your lord ——
IMOGEN.
From whom? from Leonatus?— Let me see —
Oh! learn'd indeed were that aftronomer,
That knew the ftars as I his characters ——
He'd lay the future open — You good Gods,
Let what is here contain'd relifh of love;
Of my lord's health; of his content; yet not
That we two are apart — of his content
In all but that —- good wax, thy leave — bleft bees
That make thefe locks of counfel — Good news,
    Gods.

PHILARIO.
Now let me con her vifage as fhe reads ——

IMOGEN.

(Reading) *Juftice and your father's wrath, fhould he take me in his dominions, could not be fo cruel to me, but you, oh! the deareft of creatures, would even renew me with your eyes. Take notice that I am at Milford Haven; what your own love will out of this advife you, follow. So he wifhes you all happinefs, that remains loyal to his vow, and yours increafing in love,*
                      LEONATUS.

Oh! for a horfe with wings — hear'ft thou, Philario,
He is at Milford Haven — prithee tell me

How far 'tis thither. If one of mean affairs
May plod it in a day, why may not I
Glide thither in an hour? Then, good Philario,
Who long'st like me to see thy friend; who long'st
(O let me bate) but not like me, yet long'st,
But in a fainter kind —— Oh! not like me ——
For mine's beyond, beyond —— tell me how far
To this same blessed Milford; and by the way
Tell me how Wales was made so happy as
T'inherit such a haven. But first of all,
How may we steal from hence? I prithee speak
How far to Milford?

PHILARIO.

     Madam, we may reach it,
With horses swift and sure of foot, before
The sun has ended his day's journey.

IMOGEN.

        Well ——
But how to get from hence ——

PHILARIO.

       I have a thought ——
Lady, a thousand eyes keep centinel
To watch your motions here — yet haply these
Unquestion'd we may pass — suppose you did
Assume another mien, and but disguise
That, which t'appear itself must not now be
But by self-danger — cannot you awhile
Forget to be a woman?

IMOGEN.

    I'm almost
A man already.

       PHILARIO.

PHILARIO.
Make yourself but like one,
And ev'ry gate shall kindly open to us,
Tho' Argus' self were porter.

IMOGEN.
      In my closet
I have a suit of boy's apparel ready,
That was my page's——under which disguise,
And with what imitation I can borrow
From youth of such a season, I will quit
This castle's loathsome hold.

PHILARIO.
       You are resolv'd then
To tie yourself to Leonatus' fortune,
And leave your father and the court behind you?

IMOGEN.
No court, no father now ——(for what's a father
Whose mind my crafty stepdame poison'd, that
Bore all down with her brain) no, nor no more
Of that harsh, sullen, haughty, princeling Cloten,
That Cloten, whose love-suit has been to me
As fearful as a siege.

PHILARIO.
     Hie to your chamber,
And fit you to your manhood —— dull delay
Is sin 'gainst resolution.

IMOGEN.
    I am arm'd
Ev'n for events of peril infinite,
And woman's love is courage.

         PHILARIO.

PHILARIO.
                    I will hence,
And able horse and furniture prepare
For this adventure: I'll be with you, lady,
Before you're well equipp'd.
          IMOGEN.
                    Do, good Philario:
The gracious Gods direct us!
                    [*Exeunt severally.*

End of the First ACT.

ACT II.

SCENE *The Castle*.

Enter CLOTEN *and* LORDS.

1st LORD.

IN truth, my lord, her throwing favours on
So low a thing as Leonatus is,
Slanders her judgment much; it doth substract
From her else princely qualities ⸺

CLOTEN.

     I think so ⸺

2d LORD.

Is there a spell in Leonatus' name?
What is he in his person, nature, fortune,
That you are not, and more? — Say, is he young?
You reap'd your chin since he did—is he valiant?
By Mars, you fear him not ⸺ handsome? you read
Your faithful glass with more content than he ⸺
For birth and fortune the proportion is
As top to th' bottom.

CLOTEN.

    Oh! your pardon, sir,
His lady's smile has tutor'd him a pride

That

That ranks him with the higheſt——— and though Rome
His body holds, he hath a heart and hope
In Britain ſtill; which nothing can cut off,
But ſomething that may give a mortal wound
Or to his life, or love.

Enter CYMBELINE, *and other* Lords.

1ſt LORD.
My lord, the king.
CYMBELINE.
Await you here our daughter, noble Cloten?
Will ſhe not forth?
CLOTEN.
She will vouchſafe no notice.
CYMBELINE.
The exile of her minion is too new,
She hath not yet forgot him: ſome more time
May wear the print of his remembrance out,
And then ſhe's yours.
CLOTEN.
Never, I fear, my lord.
O I have proved her heart impregnable;
I ſhould, my liege, your patience overſtretch
To tell in courſe the labours of my love;
Denials but increaſ'd my ſervices;
I have put by my nature, crouch'd and fawn'd;
I ſeem'd as if inſpir'd to do the duties
I tender'd to her; if ſhe had forſworn
All commerce with mankind, I'd been content;

But

CYMBELINE.

But Leonatus' suit had witchcraft in't,
While mine she heard as does the ruthless rock
The drowning seaman's moan.

CYMBELINE.

It must be humour:
The stubborn tendency of woman's will,
Still pliant or resisting 'gainst all rules
Of virtue and discretion —— Let her suffer ——
I have a child in thee ——

CLOTEN.

A thankful one.

CYMBELINE.

Call her before us, sirs, *(exeunt* Lords) for we would make
A last demand to her unduteous spirit,
Ere yet we take the field —— and here we swear
By the great sov'reign of th' immortal Gods,
If she consent not fully to the act,
Whereby we late have sentenc'd her divorce
From that base slave, whose vileness must not soil
The lustre of our crown, we reconfirm
Our royal grant to thee, adopted son
Of our dear love; and her blot out for ever
From all connection with our blood, and title
To this imperial diadem —— How now?

Re-enter Lords.

1st LORD.

So please you, sir, her chambers all are lock'd,
Nor answer will be given to the noise
Our loudest clamours make.

CYMBELINE.

CYMBELINE.

Hah! fled! escap'd!
How may this be?——Cloten, the guard is yours——
Have you not surety of their faith?

CLOTEN.

My liege,
They are the pick'd of my affection, and
I stand amaz'd at this.

CYMBELINE.

Where is Philario?

2d LORD.

My liege, some two hours since, I saw him take
The road that windeth round the castle grove,
And by his side a comely youth that seem'd
A page o'th' court.

CYMBELINE.

My life it must be she;
Wing'd with the fervor of her love she's flown
To Leonatus, and Philario is
The pander of her folly. We're abus'd;
All Italy in arms would hurt us less
Than what aggrieves us here——Our dear son Cloten,
Head thou the search for these vile runagates,
With thy best faculties of diligence;
Then follow to the field——We must be gone;
But we will carry our displeasure with us,
And Rome shall feel we're angry.——Come away.
[*Exeunt.*

Manet

Manet CLOTEN *with some* Lords.

To horse, sirs——mark me——I am dead to love,
And vengeance speeds me now.
[*Exit with* Lords.

SCENE *A Forest, and a Cave at a distance.*

Enter from the Cave BELLARIUS, PALADOR,
and CADWAL.

BELLARIUS.
It is a goodly sky——Stoop, boys, this gate
Instructs you how t'adore the heavens, and bows you
To ev'ning's holy office. Gates of monarchs
Are arch'd so high that giants may jut thro',
And keep their impious turbands on without
Obeisance to the sun——Hail! thou fair heav'n,
We house i' th' rock, yet use thee not so hardly
As prouder livers do.

PALADOR.
    Hail heav'n!

CADWAL.
              Hail heav'n!

BELLARIUS.
Our life, my boys, is such as mortals led
Ere living was an art. The busy knaves
That clatter in yon world, are mad to purchase
Honour with danger; wealth with envy; pleasure
With manifold infirmity; while we,
Poor in possession, in enjoyment rich,
Have no more wants than means; our av'rice is not

Wider

Wider than are our stomachs; our ambition,
Who first shall scale the steepy mountain's cliff,
Or strike the destin'd venison; this is life,
And health, the life of life.

CADWAL.

My rev'rend father,
Out of your proof you speak —— we, poor un-
fledged,
Have never wing'd from view o' th' nest, nor know
What air's from home; haply this life is best,
If quiet life is best; sweeter to you
That have a sharper known.

PALADOR.

What shall we speak of,
When we are old as you? When we shall hear
The rain and wind beat dark December, how
In this our pinching cave shall we discourse
The freezing hours away? We have seen no-
thing ——
We're beastly; subtle as the fox for prey;
Like valiant as the wolf for what we eat;
Our courage is to chace what flies; our cage
We make a choir as doth the prison'd bird,
And sing our bondage freely.

BELLARIUS.

How you speak?
Did you but know the cities' usuries,
The art o' th' court, the toil of war that goes
In quest of honest fame, yet dies i' th' search,
And hath as oft a sland'rous epitaph
As record of fair act; did you know this

CYMBELINE.

How would you smile in solitude —— Oh! boys,
The sharded beetle is in safer hold
Than is the full-wing'd eagle —— I was once
First with the best of note—Cymbeline lov'd me,
And when a soldier was the theme, my name
Was not far off —— Then was I as a tree
Whose boughs did bend with fruit; but in one night
A storm, or robb'ry, call it what you will,
Shook down my mellow hangings, nay my leaves,
And left me bare to weather.

PALADOR.
      Uncertain favour!
BELLARIUS.
My fault was nothing, (as I oft have told you)
But that two villains, sland'ring my fair honour,
Swore me confed'rate with the Romans: so
Follow'd my banishment; and these twenty
  years ——
This rock, and these demesnes have been my
  world ;
Where I have liv'd at honest freedom ; paid
More pious debts to heaven than in all
The fore-end of my time—but up to the woods—
This is not hunter's language —— He who brings
The largest fardle home is lord o' th' feast.

CADWAL.
Come, Palador —— [*Exeunt* Pal. *and* Cad.
BELLARIUS.
    I'll meet you in the valleys.
Thou divine nature, how thyself thou blazon'st

In these two princely boys! O Cymbeline!
Thy sons, tho' train'd thus meanly up among
These desart rocks, have lofty thoughts that hit
The roofs of palaces—'tis wonderful
That an invisible instinct should frame them
To royalty unlearn'd, honour untaught,
Civility not seen from others, valour
That wildly grows in them, but yields a crop,
As if it had been sow'd.———Well———I must
    after———   [*Exit*

SCENE *Another part of the Forest.*

Enter PHILARIO, *and* IMOGEN *in boy's clothes.*

IMOGEN.

Thou told'st me when we came from home, the
    place
Was near at hand. Ne'er long'd his mother so
To see him first, as I do now. Where are we?
Here is no path, no proof of habitation;
And, but we tread on solid earth, methinks
We're out o'th' bounds o'th' world———I pray,
    Philario,
Where dost thou lead me? It will soon be night,
For see the lamp of Phœbus is nigh quench'd
In Thetis' watry bosom.———

PHILARIO.
                Madam, here
Our journey ends.

IMOGEN.
          Here! where is Leonatus?

PHILARIO.

PHILARIO.
Lady, at Rome—'twere treason to be here.
IMOGEN.
Alas! what means this coldness of reply?
Hast thou abus'd me with a forged letter?
Where is my lord, Philario? —— What's the matter?
Why offer'st thou that paper to me with
A look untender? how! my husband's hand!
Quick slay, or cure me outright.
PHILARIO.
      Please you, read,
And you shall find the duty I am bound to.

IMOGEN *reads.*
My wife, Philario, hath play'd the strumpet in my bed; the testimonies whereof lie bleeding in me. I speak not out of weak surmises, but from proof, as strong as my grief, and as certain as I expect my revenge. That part, thou, Philario, must act for me; Let thine own hand take away her life; I shall give thee opportunity in the road to Milford: my letter is for that purpose to her: so, if thou fear to strike, and to certify it is done, thou hast broken thy vows, and art a traitor to friendship.

(Imogen *drops the letter, stands silent, and in the utmost consternation.*)

PHILARIO.
Is her amazement innocent or guilty?
Tell me some God,—for sure a mortal wit
May else misconstrue such perplexity.— (*Aside.*)
Madam, what cheer? are you prepar'd to die?
IMOGEN.

IMOGEN.

I false! I false to's bed? have I been chaste
As snows that sun-beam never kist, for this?
Gods! have I left my father's gilded roof,
The rights of birth, the largesses of fortune,
The pageants of pre-eminence, and all
That womanhood is said to doat on, yea
And womanhood itself?—have I left these,
No jewel taken with me but my honour,
To hear I'm false? oh! oh!

PHILARIO.

     She heeds me not.———]

IMOGEN.

False to his bed? what is it to be false?
To lie in watch there, and to think on him?
To weep 'twixt clock and clock? if sleep charge nature,
To break it with a fearful dream of him,
And cry myself awake?—that false to's bed!

PHILARIO.

What shall I do? I must be home to th' point.
          (*Aside.*)

Lady, I stand not here to try your cause:
I am your executioner:—your judge,
My friend, to whom I've sworn all offices,
Appoints me to this deed;—if thou art guilty,
I hold the sword of justice; if guilt-free,
Thy blood must light on Leonatus' head———
One pray'r and I dispatch.———

IMOGEN.

     That paper, Sir,
       Hath

Hath done the bus'ness: You may sheath your
 sword;——
I've heard I am a strumpet, and my heart
Therein false struck, can take no greater wound,
Nor tent to bottom that.
PHILARIO.
     O yet bethink you——
With what a weight descends the guilty soul,
Sunk with a load of unrepented crimes?
For such th' infernal ministers prepare
The darkest cells of Erebus.
IMOGEN.
     Nay, preach not,
But do thy work——and when thou seest my lord,
A little witness my obedience;——look——
Smiling I meet thy angry sword——come, hit
Th' innocent mansion of my love, my heart——
Prythee, dispatch——Is that the stern Philario,
That came on murder's errand?——Strike——for
 now
The lamb intreats the butcher.
PHILARIO.
     O that look
Would out-face proof. *(Aside.)* Hence thou vile
 instrument,
Thou shalt not damn my hand.——
     (Throws down the sword.)
     It cannot be
But that my friend's abus'd——some crafty villain
That's sing'lar in his art, hath done you both
This cursed injury.——O thou vip'rous slander,
     Thy

Thy edge is sharper than the murd'rous sword;
Thy tongue out-venoms all the worms of Nile;
Thy breath, that rides upon the posting winds,
Belies all corners of the world.———I'll speak
As from most firm conviction of her virtue,
To probe her still more deeply———I have yet
More test to put her to.   (*Aside.*)

IMOGEN.

                Alas! Philario,
Some jay of Italy, with painted feathers,
Hath robb'd me of his heart; poor I am stale;
A cast-off robe; a garment out of fashion;
And, for I'm richer than to hang by th' wall,
I must be ript—to pieces with me———oh!
Men's vows are women's traitors.

PHILARIO.

                      If it be so,
(As I confess it doth provoke belief)
The face of virtue shall from hence be thought
The mask of villainy; and Leonatus
Hath laid the level to all proper men;
Goodly and gallant shall be false and perjur'd,
From his great fall.

IMOGEN.

             Take up thy sword, Philario,
Behold my breast obedient as the scabbard.———
I liv'd but to one end, to do his pleasure,
And to that end would die.———

PHILARIO.

              O gracious lady,
Since I receiv'd command to do this bus'ness,
                           I scarce

I scarce have slept one wink.

IMOGEN.

Do't, and to bed then.

PHILARIO.

I'll wake mine eye-balls blind first. No, thou sweetest,
If he hath stain'd his loyalty, his mind
Is now as low to thine, as were his fortunes.——
What! shall his vileness batteries erect
To shake thy fort of innocence?—Live, lady,
To kill him with thine eye—he shall be told
That I have done his bidding, and awhile
You in some residence obscure shall 'bide,
As is thy present habit.—Come, let's hence.
Sure this discourse hath much bewilder'd me,
Or we have march'd too wide.——Fortune befriend us,
Else we have far to supper.—— This way, lady.—— [*Exeunt.*

SCENE *the Cave.*

Enter BELLARIUS.

My meditation hath misguided me,
And I have miss'd the boys. They'll not return,
Tho' all the elements should be at war,
'Till darkness sends 'em home. O Cymbeline,
When thou shalt see thy royal progeny,
(As I do mean with the first 'vantage to
Render thee back these youths) thou shalt confess

Thy lofs was gain, and thank calamity.
Hah! who are thefe?

Enter PHILARIO *and* IMOGEN.

What chance cou'd wind their fteps
Thus far from all fociety? 'tis ftrange!
        IMOGEN. *(feeing him)*
O look, Philario, look—what rev'rend figure
Is this approaches? In his vifage fits
The treafur'd wifdom of an hundred years——
The fages of old time are pictur'd thus;
Accoft him, good Philario; for his prefence
Awes my unfkilful heart.
        PHILARIO.
                Grave hermit, hail!
Pardon, old man, our ignorant intrufion,
Upon your venerable folitude.
I, and my nephew here, are bound for Milford,
And chance wide ftraying from our way to night,
Have light upon your lonely habitation.
        BELLARIUS.
Thou haft a gracious favour—for this youngling,
The dimpled God that holds the cup to Jove
Is fecond to him.—You are welcome, firs——
If you can fhape your fancy to your needs,
The wholefome viands of a homely board,
That bloated luxury ne'er cater'd to,
Shall be moft freely yours. Your names, befeech
        you?
                            PHILA-

CYMBELINE.

PHILARIO.
Philario, fir—this gentle youths' Fidele.——
BELLARIUS.
Why once more welcome—this low roof's your home,
While 'tis worth owning.—I've two fons, whofe age
Will yoke in followfhip with yours, Fidele——
Philario mates with me—tarry awhile,
And purge your lungs of the foul air o'th' city,
Or of the court, for that is fickly too——
O! I have liv'd to make the pop'lous world
A ftock for laughter.
IMOGEN.
    Uncle, we have found
Delightful lodging, and a gracious hoft——
This good old father's greeting fooths my fpirit,
Faint with this long day's march.
PHILARIO.
    Look here, Fidele——
I have a cordial of efpecial proof,
I pray thee drink it off—it is a drug
That three times hath my father's life redeem'd
From the arreft of death. It has more virtue
Than I fhall tell you now.   (*Afide.*)
IMOGEN *drinks*.
    Uncle, I thank you.
BELLARIUS.
Here come my boys.—Sirs, ftand afide awhile;
How will they take this novelty? they ne'er
Saw mortal but their mother, and myfelf.

    F 2   *Enter*

Enter PALADOR *and* CADWAL.

You, Cadwal, are best woodman, and are nam'd,
The master of the feast—hah! what are these?
Go not near, Cadwal—they are Gods that come
In visitation to our hermitage———
The eldest is God Pan; the other seems
Like swift-leg'd Mercury, or the God of Love,
Drest in his mother's smiles.—Down, Cadwal, down
On knees of adoration, and beseech
Propitious aspect from their deities———
Hear us immortal pow'rs.——— (*Kneels.*)

BELLARIUS.
Rise up my boys:
These are but mortals like ourselves, made up
Of the same stuff as we— when we have supp'd,
We will enlarge our conference.

PALADOR.
Are they men?
By the puissant Jove they're noble ones ———
I long to commune with 'em ——— for that youth
My heart is high in sudden palpitation ———
Methinks I love him neither more nor less,
Cadwal, than I do thee.

CADWAL.
Ev'n so says Cadwal.

IMOGEN.
Uncle, I have a tender feeling too,
That yearns on these fair strangers — I had once
Two brothers, whom the hand of early fate
Snatch'd

CYMBELINE.

Snatch'd from the world—If they had liv'd, I think
They had been like this gentle pair.—Sweet youths,
May I not call you brothers?

PALADOR.
Ay, most freely.
And, sir, if you are uncle to our brother,
You stand in kin to us —I pray, good father,
Let him be tutor to us: we would learn
The mystery of life; the art of war;
The policy of kings; the rules of states;
Will you instruct us? we are ign'rant yet
What drawing breath is good for.

PHILARIO.
These young plants
Are of the kindest growth my eyes e're saw——
Why, who would dream this barren desart here
A nursery of demi-gods?

BELLARIUS.
Enough;
Vice is the child of praise; my boys are such
As nature made them, and she made 'em not
For art to marr; but let us in to supper——
Our appetites shall make what's homely, sav'ry:
We eat for health, and rise before the sun,
Silvers the mountain shrubs.—Come, boys conduct
Your new compeer.—Philario, you are mine.——

PALADOR.
The night to th' owl, and morn to th' lark less
welcome. [*Exeunt into the cave.*

End of the Second ACT.

ACT. III.

Enter PHILARIO *from the Cave.*

HOW restless is this thinking! welcome day!
Now I shall sift her thoroughly—for what's past
Little hangs on it——were she true and artless,
Thus would she'have; if false and artful, thus—
She shall be told in words as strong and hateful,
As earnestness can make 'em, what she drank
Is deadly to all sense, as for a time
It is, to full effect.——'Tis a rare drug
That locks the spirits up in shew of death,
To be more fresh reviving——Dread of death
Shall force me out the truth; fraud will be honest
Itself thus over-reach'd——but hist, Bellarius.

Enter BELLARIUS.

Our courtiers say all's savage but at court—
How does this hospitable rock, Bellarius,
Give 'em the lie?

BELLARIUS.

Our minds must not be measur'd
By this rude place we live in—You are rouz'd
Before the hunter's hour—Could you not sleep
Upon your bed of moss?

Before

CYMBELINE. 39

PHILARIO.
                    Ay, fir, as foundly
As cradled infancy.
            BELLARIUS.
                    Your chamber was
The beft o'th' houfe—For us we often make
The ftar-wrought sky our tefter—Wearinefs
Can fnore upon the flint, when refty floth
Finds the down pillow hard—what think you, fir,
Of this our way of life?
            PHILARIO.
                    It is unknown,
And therefore envied not—our courtly great ones
May blufh at their high breeding; here's the place
Where virtue teaches fchool—are your fons up?
By Jove multipotent there's not a couple,
Whofe praife fame trumpets with her loud'ft O yes,
That can out-peer thefe twain—they feem as gentle
As Zephyrs blowing 'neath the hyacinth,
Not wagging his fweet head, and yet as rough
(Their fprightly blood by a good tale once warm'd)
As the rude wind that by the top doth take
The mountain pine, and make him ftoop to th' vale.——
            BELLARIUS.
Why, thou haft mark'd them well—Lo! where they come,
And with 'em your Fidele.

Enter

Enter PALADOR, CADWAL, *and* IMOGEN.

BELLARIUS.

So, my boys,
Are your devotions to the morning star
With solemn homage paid?

PALADOR.

They are, my father.

BELLARIUS.

What says Fidele? Can he like a court
No bigger than this cave?

IMOGEN.

Believe me, sir,
The partnership of labour here, is richer
Than golden honours there.

CADWAL.

I've said I love thee—
I cannot say how much, but sure as much
As I do love my father——

BELLARIUS.

What? How? How?

PALADOR.

If it be sin to say so, sir, I join me
In my good brother's fault—I know not why
I love this youth, and I have heard you say
Love reasons without reason. Fate at door,
And a demand who is't shall die, I'd say
My father, not this youth——

BELLARIUS.

'Tis wonderful:
Does instinct tell them I am not their father?
(*Aside.*)

CYMBELINE. 41

Well—to the field—tis the fourth hour o'th' morn.
Philario, and Fidele will remain
Here in the cave—We'll come to you after hunt-
    ing;
Or are you for our sport?

IMOGEN.
              I am not well——
A sudden laziness creeps o'er my senses,
As if fatigue acknowledg'd no repair
By this nights' sleep——

PHILARIO.
          The drug begins to work—
                      (*Aside.*)

PALADOR.
Go you to hunting—I'll abide with him.

IMOGEN.
No—to your journal course—the breach of custom
Is breach of all—My uncle will stay here—
Farewel—I wish you sport—I shall be well
By your return——

ALL.
          We'll not be long away.—
[*Exeunt* Bellarius, Palador, *and* Cadwal.

PHILARIO.
These are kind creatures, lady.

IMOGEN.
                On my life
I'd change my sex to be companion with 'em,
Since my dear lord is false.

PHILARIO.
              I would confer
Once more upon that theme.
                              I'm

IMOGEN.

      I'm sick already;
And would you minister fresh pain, Philario?

PHILARIO.
Come—I'll no more dissemble—you are known
False to your banish'd lord.

IMOGEN.
      What hear I, Gods!

PHILARIO.
The truth, the killing truth—art not asham'd?
—But shame is masculine—Could I find out
The woman's part in me—for there's no motion
That tends to vice in man, but I affirm
It is the woman's part; be't lying, note it,
The woman's flatt'ring, yours; deceiving, yours;
Lust and rank thoughts, yours, yours; revenges,
   yours;
Ambition; covetings; change of prides; disdain;
Nice longings; slanders; mutability;
All faults that may be nam'd, nay, that hell
   knows,
Why yours in part, or all; but rather all——
For ev'n to vice
You are not constant, but are changing still
One vice but of a minute old, for one
Not half so old as that.

IMOGEN.
     Am I awake?
Or have you senses perfect?

PHILARIO.
                'Tis enough——
I have atchieved more than er'e did Julius,
And will be chronicled 'mongſt thoſe wiſe few
That have out-craftied woman.
IMOGEN.
                    You amaze me.
PHILARIO.
Oh! no more fooling—I have proof that tells
The time, the place, the—fie upon it, lady,
It wounds my modeſty to quote the deeds
That coſt thee not a bluſh.
IMOGEN.
                Blaſphemer, hold!
Thou art in league with perjur'd Leonatus,
And doſt traduce a lady that deſpiſes
Malice and thee like.
PHILARIO.
        Go to—you're naught—
IMOGEN.
Villain, your proof? Why ſtand you idle thus?
If thou do'ſt ſee a ſpeck upon my honour,
Prick at it with the ſword, your juſt remorſe
E'en now let drop.
PHILARIO.
          Miſtake not, lady mine,
Remorſe was counterfeit, my purpoſe real;
I found you paſt all grace, and did commence
Cunning in my revenge; your puniſhment

Were nothing if not such; you have your death,
Yet never felt his sting.

IMOGEN.
What says Philario!

PHILARIO.
O now you tremble like a guilty soul
Beneath the furies lash——now you would pour
A deluge of salt grief to wash your crimes——
It is too late, thou hast out-liv'd repentance——
That draught was tinctured with a mortal juice,
And he that drinks an acron on't, is serv'd,
As I would serve a dog.

IMOGEN.
Sir, my surprize
Relishes not of fear.——This is a cure
Which you do call a chastisement——I feel
The death thou speak'st of curdling in my veins.——
How sweetly do they sleep whom sorrow wakes
not!
Farewel——my innocence is sacrifice,
Or to the blindfold rage of jealousy,
Or to estranged love——O Leonatus,
The Gods have pity on thee.

PHILARIO.
Do I speak?
Is this my hand? are these my eyes?——All this
I will to question put, if thou art true——
O Imogen, but that I thought thee foul,
And thy confession a superfluous warrant,
I would have ta'en my sucking infant's throat,

And

CYMBELINE.

And broach'd it with my martial fcymeter,
E're touch'd thy precious life.

IMOGEN.

I do forgive thee—
Thy judgment (which how warp'd it matters not)
Condemn'd me to this death—Nay, weep not, fir,
Commend me to my lord—alas! Philario,
I grieve myfelf to think how much hereafter,
When the belief, or falfe affection, which
Holds pris'ner now his mind, fhall leave him free,
His mem'ry will be pang'd by looking back
On my hard cafe of woe—my brain is heavy—

PHILARIO.

The mighty Gods throw ftones of fulphur on
All jealous, head-fick fools—He faw it not—
And ev'ry day's experience doth difprove
The ftrong'ft report—O the accurfed fate
That damn'd me to this office——

IMOGEN.

Curb thy rage
Unprofitably loos'd—I'll in, and die——
Follow me not—my foul has that to do
Which is beft done in fecret—fare thee well——
Prefent to our good hoft, and my fweet brothers,
My thanks and choiceft bleffings.

[*Exit.* Imogen *into the Cave.*

PHILARIO.

It goes well,
Her honour I have fann'd, and found it chaffleſs—
Friend, thou art fool, or villain—If I prove
Thou would'ft betray my love to purpofes

Of hell-black colour, tho' our friendship stood
Upon a brazen base, it should dissolve,
And, like the film that dews the morning flower,
Break into unseen air.   Hah Palador!——

Enter PALADOR *hastily*

Lend me thy sword, good Uncle——as I crost
The mountain's ridge, a fellow at a distance
(Whose drapery by far out-glistens thine)
Bad me with accents stern and masterly
Stop and attend his speech—I hied me hither,
And, if he follow, will responses make
By word, or blow, an he dare question me——
Belike 'tis talk'd at court that such as we
Cave here ; haunt here ; are outlaws ; and in time
May make some stronger head ; the which he hearing
Is sworn with choice attendants in his train
To fetch us in—It is a crisis that
My father sometimes drops discourses of.——

PHILARIO.
Say'st so ? I will go climb the rock, and spie
What companies are near.   [*Exit.* Philario.

PALADOR.
                Do—for this bravo,
Let me alone with him——this instrument
Fits my hand well—I grasp it fast as tho'
'Twere part of me, and grew unto my arm——
I feel I can do any thing but fear——
I will look out.——By the broad shield of Mars

He

CYMBELINE. 47

He comes unto my wish——up sword, and sleep
Till I awake thee, hap'ly soon——

Enter CLOTEN.

CLOTEN.
       My zeal
Hath far out-gone my train—hark thee—thou fellow,
Why didst thou fly me? didst not hear me call?

PALADOR.
I did, and therefore came not.

CLOTEN.
      Saucy hind——
Thou art some villain mountaineer——What art thou?

PALADOR.
A man—thou look'st as if thou cam'st from court,
And yet thou art no more.

CLOTEN.
      Thou know'st me not—
Answer me, wretch, on peril of thy life——
Saw'st thou two trav'lers speeding thro' the forest—
The elder somewhat 'bove my age, the younger
Few years below your own?

PALADOR.
     Such if I saw,
I saw 'em not for thee——

CLOTEN.
     Ha! dost thou mock me?
Where are the traitors, slave? quick, or——

PALA-

PALADOR.
A thing
More flavish did I ne'er, than anfwering
A flave, without a blow.

CLOTEN.
Thou art a robber;
A law-breaker; a villain; yield thee, thief —

PALADOR.
To whom? to thee? what art thou? Have not I
An arm as big as thine? a heart as big?
Thy words I grant are bigger — for I wear not
My dagger in my mouth — fay what thou art,
Why I fhould yield to thee?

CLOTEN.
Thou villian bafe!
Know'ft me not by my garb?

PALADOR.
No, nor thy tailor ———
Who is thy grandfather? — he made that garb,
Which, as it feems, makes thee ———

CLOTEN.
Injurious thief!
Hear but my name, and tremble ———

PALADOR.
What's thy name?

CLOTEN.
Cloten, thou villain!

PALADOR.
Cloten? then double villain be thy name;
I cannot tremble at it; were it Toad,
Adder, or Spider, it would move me fooner——

CLOTEN.

CYMBELINE. 49

CLOTEN.
Then to thy fear, and mere confusion, know
I'm son to the late queen, and heir to th' crown.
PALADOR.
In troth I'm sorry for't; thyself not seeming
So worthy as thy birth.—Me thou hast wrong'd,
Tho' thou wert son of Juno.
CLOTEN.
     Thou vile thing!
Wrong thee!—But die the death—thou wilt be honour'd
To perish by this hand—when I have slain thee,
I'll on the gate of Lud's Town set thy head
To roast i'th' sun.   (*Drawing.*)
PALADOR.
   Are you for scratching? Come——
To-day I'll lose a soldier's maidenhead ——
Hah! are you down? I see a prince is made (*fight*)
Of penetrable stuff———   (Cloten *falls.*)
CLOTEN.
  Dog! thou hast slain me. (*dies.*)
PALADOR.
Ay, and the world no loser——This is sport
Hotter than hunting——I will kill no more
The tim'rous deer——such killing's cowardice—
My reeking sword sweats honourably now ——
Thou poor loud-boasting fool! Hah! how I stalk
In triumph round thee! like the victor lion
Slow pacing 'bout the mangled tyger's corse,
And grimly taking solace in his slaughter——

    H   *Enter*

Enter BELLARIUS, CADWAL, *and* PHILARIO.
BELLARIUS.
I heard the clash of swords —— O Palador!
What hast thou done?
PALADOR.
I'm perfect what—— cut thro' one Cloten's heart,
Son to the queen, after his own report ——
He came in search of thee and fair Fidele,
Or I did much misconstrue his demand ——

(*To* Philario.

He call'd me villain, mountaneer, and swore
He would displace my head, where now it grows,
And set it on Lud's Town.
PHILARIO.
'Tis very Cloten,
The king's adopted son.
PALADOR.
Why had the king
Misus'd bold Palador, his royalty
Had lain so weltring there —— What company
Discover you abroad?
PHILARIO.
No single soul
Can I set eye on—yet 'tis strange his anger
Should bring him here alone.
BELLARIUS.
I'll not believe
But quick revenge pursues us!
PALADOR.
Let it come;
Let it be such as possible strength may meet,
It shall be welcome.
CADWAL.

CYMBELINE.

CADWAL.
That's my valiant brother ⸺
Thou hast said well, done well; O Palador!
I love thee brotherly, but envy much
Thou'st rob'd me of this deed. Where's sweet
    Fidele?

PHILARIO.
Asleep within the cave. — Hear me, good sirs —
This act, I trust, is dangerless, except
We're traitors to ourselves.—Boys, take the body,
And let it down the creek behind the rock
Into the sea   (*Exeunt* Pal. *and* Cad. *with the body.*)
    Bellarius, hark a word ⸺
Thy sons are noble ones, and pity 'tis
Their worth should waste in dull obscurity.
To day fell war unfurls his bloody flag
Between the Roman and the British host,
And confidence is goad to either side.
Upon the border of the forest here,
The Roman lies encamp'd—and two hours march
Will join our countrymen — your valiant boys
May, in such fight as this is like to prove,
Begin and end a fame.

BELLARIUS.
        Why now or never
'Tis fit they launch into the world, Philario,
But fitter never.

PHILARIO
    Do not say so, sir;
Britain doth lack such hearts.

BELLARIUS.
        Well, you shall rule me —

Indeed I wish'd for such a day as this,
To make them known to Cymbeline. *(aside.)*
    They're here.

Enter PALADOR *and* CADWAL.
PALADOR.
We've sent him down the stream, and so to sea,
To tell the fishes he's the queen's son Cloten.——
BELLARIUS.
My boys, your uncle here would steal you from me,
To your bruis'd country's wars.
PALADOR.
                      Oh! let us go;
For this hath been our daily fervent prayer——
Uncle, intreat again — why I can fight —
You have to-day a sample — so can Cadwal——
Our opposition we will stake 'gainst two,
The stoutest of old Rome——ay, against odds,
If valour's scarce in Britain.
CADWAL.
                      Odds to chuse.
BELLARIUS.
The king hath wrong'd me — he deserveth not
Your service, and my love.
PALADOR.
                  The king's deservings
I weigh not now——this is a public cause.
I do not know my countrymen, but know
They were not born to be the slaves of Rome,
To wear the badge of foreign tyranny,
And crouch to aliens that dominion hold
By rape, not right ——
                            PHILARIO.

CYMBELINE.

PHILARIO.
     O! such a spirit as this
Will drive the pestilent invasion hence,
And post it short-breath'd home.
  PALADOR.
       Why, my good uncle,
Why not pursue it at the heels, and pay
The foe in kind—Let the hot war return
Upon our enemies heads.—O! for the time,
When Britons bold shall throng the streets of
  Rome,
And breathe strange climes, that conquest makes
  our own.
  PHILARIO.
Most like a Briton said.—To-day shall put
This courage to more proof.
  PALADOR.
      Sir, I will fight
For liberty, and Britain, till the blood
Be drain'd thro' all my veins; and when my arm
Has lost his office, I will to the last
Give token of resistance.
  CADWAL.
     So will I;
I am asham'd to look upon the sun,
To have the benefit of his blest beams
So long a poor unknown: Sure than be so
Better to cease to be.
  BELLARIUS.
     Have with you boys!
No reason I, since of your lives you set

         So

So flight a valuation, fhou'd referve
My crack'd one to more care.—We'll all to the army.
Philario and Fidele fhall keep houfe,
Till our return.

PHILARIO.
Not fo Bellarius; we
Habited like yourfelf, to 'fcape the eye
Of knowledge, will atteft to day the feats
Of thefe brave lads.

PALADOR.
Why, let the Gods be witnefs,
And celebrate this birth-day of our glory——
Liberty!

CADWAL.
Britain!

BOTH.
Liberty and Britain!

BELLARIUS.
Go, fee if young Fidele be awake.
[*Exeunt* Palador *and* Cadwal.
Doth not this mettle promife well, Philario?
I fcarce wou'd change a fon with Jupiter!
The fervice of thefe lufty boys fhall do
The king more good, than this fame Cloten's death
Hath done him harm.—(*Solemn mufic within.*)
Hah! wherefore founds within
My moft ingenious inftrument? What caufe
Should give it motion now?

Enter

CYMBELINE.

Enter PALADOR.

PALADOR.

       The bird is dead
That we have made so much on. O come in
And see what violent hands stern death has laid
Upon the sweetest lily of the land.——

     (They go into the Cave.)

SCENE *opens and discovers the inside of the Cave, with* Bellarius, Philario, Paladar, *and* Cadwal, *round the Body of* Imogen, *lying upon a Couch of Moss.*

PHILARIO.

Alas! my dearest nephew!

PALADOR.

      I had rather
Have leap'd from twenty years of age to eighty,
And turn'd my warlike spear into a crutch,
Than have seen this.

BELLARIUS.

O poor Fidele! Jove doth know what man
Thou might'st have made—thou died'st a most
  rare boy.
Tell us how found you him?

PALADOR.

     Stark as you see;
And smiling thus, as if the dart of death
Had gently tickl'd slumber;

CADWAL.

     O sweet brother,
With female fairies will thy tomb be haunted,
And worms shall not come near thee.——

PALADOR.

>   With fair flow'rs
> (While summer lasts, and I live here, Fidele)
> I will adorn thy grave —— Thou shalt not lack
> The flow'r that's like thy face, pale primrose; nor
> The azur'd harebell like thy veins; no nor
> The leaf of eglantine, which, not to slander't,
> Out-sweeten'd not thy breath—The ruddock would
> With charitable bill bring thee all this,
> Yea and furr'd moss besides, when flow'rs were none,
> To winter-gown thy corse. ——

BELLARIUS.

>   Come, boys, have done,
> And play no more in wench-like words with that
> Which is so serious — Hence, and lay his corps
> Near good Euriphile's, your worthy mother's —

PALADOR.

> Be't so — but, Cadwal, first, albeit thy voice
> Has now the mannish crack, sing o'er his body
> In note and words like those which thou didst chaunt
> O'er good Euriphile —— e'er she was lodg'd
> Within her leafy grave——Come on—begin—

The DIRGE.

Set by Mr. ARNE, *sung by Mr.* LOWE.

Fear no more the heat o' th' sun,
  Nor the furious winter's blast;
Thou thy worldly task hast done,
  And the dream of life is past.

Golden

CYMBELINE.

Golden lads and girls all muſt
Follow thee, and come to duſt.

Fear no more the frown o' th' great,
  Death doth mock the tyrant foe;
Happieſt is the early fate,
  Miſery with time doth grow.
Monarchs, ſages, peaſants muſt
Follow thee, and come to duſt.

  No exorciſer harm thee!
  No ſpell of witchcraft charm thee!
  Grim ghoſt unlaid forbear thee!
  The fairy elves be near thee!
    Quiet conſummation have,
    Unremoved be thy grave.

BELLARIUS.
Theſe are our rural obſequies, Philario ——
PHILARIO.
Moſt ſweet and ſolemn, ſir.
BELLARIUS.
When you've remov'd the body, back repair
Here to the cave, and fit you for the field.
—We'll ſhare our little armory among us ——
And, ſons, e'er ev'ning we'll forget this grief,
And wipe our tear-ſtain'd cheeks with bloody
    hands.
—— Come, good Philario ——
              [*Exeunt ſeverally.*

End of the Third ACT.

ACT IV.

SCENE *A Field of Battle.*

Enter CYMBELINE, LORDS, &c.

CYMBELINE.

THINK you the Roman will not quit his ground,
And meet our battle in the open plain?

1st LORD.

So please your grace, it is my faith he will;
We are already beaten in conceit,
And pride does still forego his 'vantages.
Best then halt here, my liege.

CYMBELINE.

Halt! give the word.

(*Within*) Halt! halt! halt! halt!

CYMBELINE.

Our son not yet return'd! Oh! here comes one
That was a limb o'th' party. What now, captain?

Enter an Officer.

OFFICER.

My liege, prince Cloten far outstripp'd his train,
And we're to seek the seeker——His spurr'd horse
We found upon the verge of yonder forest,
But him no tidings speak of.

CYMBELINE.
>   Take thou his charge,
> And so bestir thee in the field, that none
> May think his valour missing. Well—how now?

Enter another Officer.

OFFICER.
> My liege, here are without four volunteers
> That seem to promise marvels, tho' their looks
> And garb be such as hermits wont to wear
> In most retired sequestration;
> They have bewitch'd the soldier's hearts, and crave
> Instant admittance to your Majesty.

CYMBELINE.
> It doth amaze us —— let 'em come before us —
> [*Exit* Lord, *and returns with* Bellarius,
>   Palador, Cadwal, *and* Philario.
> Now by the arm of Jove a comely sight,
> Those silver locks are taxers of respect
> Tho' kings be lookers on —— All welcome,
>   strangers ——
> Whence and what are you?

BELLARIUS.
>   Mighty Cymbeline,
> Hermits we are, that have a homely dwelling
> Where want keeps house—— yet are we bold to boast
> Our hands and hearts as good as any he's,
> That dares look Roman in the face.

CYMBELINE.

CYMBELINE.
Thy speech
Gives earneſt of much worth —— Say, who are theſe
The colleagues of your enterprize?

BELLARIUS.
Dread ſir,
Theſe ſtriplings are my ſons; this worthy fellow
Is kinſman of my wife's ——

PALADOR.
Firſt, let's go fight,
And then to telling tales.

CYMBELINE.
So prompt, ſo young!
Waſt thou a ſoldier born? Is warlike ſcience
By inſpiration caught, which ſtill we judg'd
By long experience learn'd?

BELLARIUS.
O royal ſir,
My boys are of a gen'rous breed —— Great Gods,
When on my three-foot ſtool I ſit, and tell
The val'rous feats I've done, (for I am free
Of this ſame trade of war) how will this youth,
My firſt-born Palador, let his ſpirits fly
Out at my ſtory? "Thus mine enemy fell,
"And thus (ſay I) I ſet my foot on's neck—"
Ev'n then the blood flows in his cheeks, he ſweats,
Strains his young nerves, and puts himſelf in poſture
That acts my words —— His younger brother Cadwal

CYMBELINE. 61

With ardour emulous, and as like a figure,
Strikes life into my speech; and richly shews
His great conceiving.

CYMBELINE.
      In a time that look'd
More perilous than this, such early virtue
Would bode us issue fortunate to Britain ——

Enter another Officer *in haste.*

Soldier thy speed is big with consequence ——
Proclaim it with thy tongue ——
OFFICER.
      To arms, my liege,
The Roman legions are come down the hill,
And their loud clarions sound to present battle.
CYMBELINE.
Thanks for thy news —— Return the slaves de-
 fiance;   *(sound within.)*
Stretch your big hearts, my countrymen, and shout
From the strong lungs of liberty, till air
Waft your incessant clamours to the thrones
Of the admiring Gods. *(a great shout.)* Remem-
 ber, sirs,
We go to fight for death, or victory.——
O let us only live on terms of conquest!
Who dies, at least dies free-man, blessed dies
To live immortal in his country's songs ——
If there's a coward here, let him post back
To his soft bed and caudle——I should weep
Worse than a love-sick girl to find to-day
          Our

Our hearts not of a piece —— Come on, brave fellows,
For soldiers all are fellows —— We'll yet live
(Unless my sins abuse my divination)
To see old Lud's Town bright with joyful fires,
And Britons strut in triumph —— Set we on —
[*Exeunt.*

Alarum. Enter LEONATUS *in disguise.*

They go to battle with a jocund spirit ——
But ah! how heavy is his heart, who bears
A bosom-war within him? O Philario,
(For I well know thy friendship such, thou'st done
The letter of my will) thou should'st have paus'd —
Anger is indiscreet in his commands ——
Too true, the noble Imogen did wrong me;
(And so, I doubt not, did my mother him
I call'd my father, tho' she still was held
The non-pareil of virtue) yet her fault,
The nat'ral failing of her sex, not hers,
Was ill pusu'd with vengeance capital
By me —— O Britain, I have kill'd my wife,
Who was thy mistress —— therefore thus array'd
Like a poor soldier, neither known, nor guess'd at,
Pitied or hated, to the face of peril
Myself I'll dedicate —— Heav'n knows my life
Is ev'ry breath a death.

Alarum. Fight. Enter CYMBELINE *and* Romans.
CYMBELINE *is in danger of being slain, or taken.*
Then enter LEONATUS *and rescues him.*

LEONATUS.

CYMBELINE.

LEONATUS.

What have we here? The majesty of Britain
O'erpower'd by odds —— Room for an honest sword
That loyalty gives edge to —— how they fly
When resolution drives 'em.—— *(the* Romans *fly.)*

CYMBELINE.

                Great, tho' mean ——
Noble obscure, we thank thee —— what's thy name?

LEONATUS.

I cannot stay to tell thee —— hear'st thou not
How loud Mars bellows yonder? — only this ——
The king has friends he knows not —— fare you well,
My sword will cool else.—— [*Exit* Leonatus.

CYMBELINE.

                What blunt fellow's this?
We have no time to wonder —— How now, captain?

Enter an Officer.

OFFICER.

Advance, my liege —— Our battle galls 'em sorely ——
Yon sage, and his boy-hermits fight like dragons.
The Roman eagle flaps his wing for flight,
And conquest smiles upon us.

CYMBELINE.

Follow me;
And still the word be, Cymbeline, and Britain
[*Exeunt.*

Alarum. Fight. Enter Britons *and* Romans *fighting. The* Romans *give back. Then enter, at opposite doors,* PISANIO, *and* PALADOR.

PALADOR.

It is a jovial chace——fight on, young Cadwal,
Thou shalt go halves in glory—— I could swear
To go to bed no more—Well met, thou Roman,
I have been killing vermin —— thou dost seem
Worthy my sword —— Art thou of blood and honour?

PISANIO.

Away, and save thy life, thou swagg'ring boy,
By Romulus, my vengeance would not stoop
(Albeit a thousand souls are groaning for't)
To such a lout as thee.

PALADOR.

Hah! didst thou learn
Thy valour at a dancing school?—— I'll try
Your lightsomness of foot —— Fool, I will hunt thee
E'en to thy master's throne.——

PISANIO.

Come on, rash hind ——
(*Fight*, Pisanio *falls.*)
Thou hast o'erpower'd me stripling —— the just Gods

Unbrac'd

Unbrac'd my arm—the heaviness of guilt
Took off my manhood—I've bely'd a lady,
The princess of this country; and the air on't
Revengingly enfeebled me; brave youth,
Witness the penance of my dying hour,
And let the noble Leonatus know
I crav'd in death his pardon——

PALADOR.
How is this? Roman, proceed.

PISANIO.
I was confederate with
Cloten (than whom a viler wretch not lives
'Twixt sky and ground)

PALADOR.
Nay, by the Gods, he lives not;
I slew him but to-day, and sure e're this
He is the food of sharks.

PISANIO.
Thou hast the arm
That heav'n does justice with—I can no more—
Take thou this note of Cloten's *(gives a note)* it doth speak
In terms full relative to the device
Then hatching in his brain; and farther marks
The lowly bendings of his love to Cæsar——
This shall confirm thy by-and-by report
Strongly as living evidence——I've done
More good in my last hour, than can be pick'd
From my whole piece of life——there's hope in that,
And in that hope I die—— *(dies)*

PALADOR.

Nay, if thou hop'ſt,
I'll write deſpair down folly——Jupiter,
What a vile rogue was this? and yet he wore
A worthy ſeeming——I perceive my garb
Doth ſhame the guiſe o'th' world——I will ſet out
New faſhion; leſs without, and more within.
What have we here? *(Flouriſh.)*

Enter LEONATUS.

LEONATUS.

Hermit, our wars are done;
The Romans turn their backs, and victory
To-day is wedded to great Cymbeline.
O that the joy of all ſhould touch not me!
I am not mortal ſure; for death I ſought,
Yet found him not where I did hear him groan,
Nor felt him where he ſtruck. This ugly monſter,
'Tis ſtrange he hides him in freſh cups, ſmooth beds,
Sweet words, and hath more miniſters than we
That draw his knives in war.

PALADOR.

Art thou a Briton,
And doſt not laugh to-day? Sad looks are treaſon,
And take the part of Rome; the man that feels
His own diſtreſs, hates more his pers'nal grief,
Than he doth love his country.

CYMBELINE.

LEONATUS.
O you know not—
Hah! who lies there? Ye Gods, it is Pisanio—
The damn'd Italian fiend that stain'd my honour;
I would have sav'd an hundred lives in fight
To have met his.

PALADOR.
If thou art Leonatus,
(As by thy talk thou should'st be) I have matter
For your quick hearing.

LEONATUS.
I am Leonatus,
I would I were aught else!

PALADOR.
That villain there
Did much abuse you, Sir.

LEONATUS.
He did abuse me
Beyond the pow'r of all his worthless tribe
To make amends—Who robs me of my wealth,
May one day have ability, or will
To yield me, full repayment——but the villain
That doth invade a husband's right in bed,
Is murd'rer of his peace, and makes a breach
In his life's after-quiet, that the grief
Of penitence itself cannot repair.

PALADOR.
Thou dost mistake thy woe, good Leonatus,
Which yet (if the great Gods are merciful)
I have a cure for——

LEONATUS.
How! where! which way! when!

PALADOR.
Sir, your belief in your dear lady's truth
Is falsely wounded, who, be sure (for aught
This arch impostor Roman could disprove)
Has kept her bond of chastity uncrack'd,
And is as cold as Dian.
LEONATUS.
     Ay, and colder;
For Dian is alive——If thou not fool'st me,
Thou curest common sickness with the plague,
And killest with relief——I could not find
The virtue of my wife untainted now,
(That once I priz'd to adoration)
For the best carbuncle of Phœbus' wheel,
Nay, all the worth of's car.
PALADOR.
     Alas! I'm sorry
Your much wrong'd judgment hath proceeded
   thus.——
For free and full confession made this wretch
Of most refined stratagem to change
Your biass of affection: Sir, this note,
Which with his dying hand he did bequeath you,
Will more at large illustrate what my tongue
Faulters in utt'rance of. *(gives the note.)*
LEONATUS.
     Quick, let me see it,
Impatient misery longs to know the worst,
E'en when the worst is fatal. *(reads)*
 The Lord Cloten *to the* Roman *Knight* Pisanio.
Cloten! the name is ominous——it bodes
More than the raven's sullen flap that scents
Cadaverous infirmity.——But on—— *If*

CYMBELINE. 69

If thou lov'st me, let me see thee ere night. I have bought the fidelity of the princess's woman with my gold; she will give thee admittance into her chamber, when nothing will be awake but anger and policy; where thou may'st make such note as will be sufficient to the madding of the abhorred Leonatus. Thy service herein will tie me closer to thyself, and to Augustus thy lord. No more till thou dost console with thy presence, thine and Cæsar's in affection, CLOTEN.

PALADOR.
How fare you, sir? Alack! his grief is dumb.

LEONATUS.
Are there no Gods? or are they Gods that sleep,
And leave us to ourselves?—Oh! I have done it—
I've reach'd the point of shame, and villainy
Is less than 'twas.——Twice doubly curst be he
That first did graff the failings of his wife
On a fool's head's suspicion.—I've destroy'd
The temple of fair virtue, yea herself———
Spit, and throw stones, cast mire upon me, set
The dogs o'th' street to bait me; ev'ry fool
Be Leonatus call'd. O! Imogen,
My queen, my love my wife, oh! Imogen!

PALADOR.
Mark thou unhappy Briton, how my soul
Catches thy grief——my eyes half drown my tongue.
Wife—what is wife? what is it thou dost feel?
The pang that gripes thee seems more keen than mine was,
When my good mother, and Fidele died!
——Yet

—Yet then I mourn'd heart-deep—O that thy woes
Had remedy within the reach of power,
I would purſue endeavours infinite
'Till raſhneſs ſhould be virtue. Pardon me
This vain, vain boaſt——Valour himſelf muſt weep
When he cannot redreſs—I'll ſit down by thee,
And mourn 'till I beguile thee of thy ſorrows—
We'll give our ſhares in this day's triumph up
To riot and hard-hearted jollity.
O Imogen, where art thou?—ſoft—here comes
Philario, my good uncle.

Enter PHILARIO.

LEONATUS.
How! Philario?
O turn a thouſand Romans looſe upon me,
But ſhew me not Philario.
PHILARIO.
Palador,
Have we a madman here?
LEONATUS.
Ay, of thy making.
Thou cred'lous fool, egregious murtherer,
Thief, any thing, that's due to villains paſt,
In being, or to come.———
PHILARIO.
I know thee not.
LEONATUS.
Know'ſt thou not Leonatus?
PHILARIO.

CYMBELINE.

PHILARIO.
       Art thou he?
And doſt thou greet me thus?
LEONATUS.
       Where is my wife?
My wife, my wife, my Imogen, thou villain!
PHILARIO.
Baſe and ungrateful! is it come to this?
Have I then offer'd up my mind's repoſe,
My better judgment, and my nature's pity,
To thy injunction? Have I ſtain'd my ſword
With blood as rich as ever yet did waſh
A Britiſh heart, to be bequeſtion'd now
With, villain, where's my wife, my Imogen?
——But that thy will was abſolute herein,
I could have wiſh'd the damned charge had aim'd
At univerſal ruin of the ſex,
And her alone left out.
LEONATUS.
     I'm wild——forgive me;
I've kill'd my wife, and ſhall my friend eſcape
Th' abuſes of my fury?——Read, Philario,
Read this black ſcroll, *(gives him the letter)* read
   it, and after tell me,
If jealouſy be written in the liſt
Of ſins that mercy reaches.
PHILARIO.
       You're undone;
And ſo am I——come not to me for comfort,
For my own pers'nal grief out-meaſures all
The patience I was born with.
LEONATUS.

CYMBELINE.

LEONATUS.

Patience! who
Is patient in despair? Can patience wake
The sleep of death? Can it command old time
To render back the hours he snatch'd away,
Or what is done, make undone? Give me cord,
Poison, or knife, some upright justicer,
And then prescribe me patience.

PALADOR.

O Bellarius,
Thy lectures all were true, and this world holds
Nothing but woe and villainy—where's Cadwal?
We'll homeward to the rock.———

PHILARIO.

Hold thee, young man———
The king must thank you for your services———
Anon he will be here; and, Leonatus,
Do not, I pray, with rashness over-ripe
A vi'lence on thyself———best wait we both
The royal sentence on our lives, and die
Without more folly on our heads———to me
The op'ning leave of this.

LEONATUS.

Well, let me die———
The rest you shall command—I see her now—
Bloody and pale she looks———her snow-white breast
Whose fragrance sent up incense to the Gods,
Is soil'd with clotted gore———her jetty locks,
Where Cupid and a thousand graces play'd,
Are turn'd to fury's snakes———and in her eye,
At whose kind beams glad Hymen light his torch,

Sits

CYMBELINE.

Sits fiery vengeance now with direful looks
Chilling my faculties.

PHILARIO.
     If thou art man,
Be like one now—die as a foldier fhould do,
And do not ftart at fhadows—I've bethought me
How we may fit and full difclofure make
Of all our purpofes to Cymbeline;
Yea, and of Cloten's too, (whereof the truth
Shall the king's heart fore fmite) that devil Cloten
Of whom this gallant youth has well reveng'd us.

LEONATUS.
Has he? who, what art thou, thou wond'rous man!
To whom I am indebted for the fcourge
Of my two deadly foes.

PHILARIO.
    He is a wonder
Myfelf can fcarce explain;—But hark, the king.—
        (*Flourish.*)
Let us, my wretched friend, appear a while,
What our now-habits fpeak us.

Enter CYMBELINE, BELLARIUS, CADWAL, Lords,
and Soldiers.

CYMBELINE.
     Thanks to all;
Chiefly to you, whom the great Gods have made
Beft pillars of my throne. Where are the reft?
O here's your worthy kinfman, your brave fon,
And the poor foldier that in rags did fhame

CYMBELINE.

Rich coats of war, and with his naked breast
Stept before shields of proof——we owe our life
To his true valour.

BELLARIUS.
I did never see
Such noble fury in so mean a thing;
Such precious deeds in one that promis'd nought
But begg'ry and bad luck.

CYMBELINE.
All bow your knees—
*(Bellarius, Philario, Palador, Cadwal
and Leonatus kneel.)*

Arise, my knights o'th' battle; we create you
Companions to our person, and will give you
Estates becoming your new dignities.

PALADOR.
My Lord, the honour I have won to-day
Is sustenance for me——I fought for fame,
And riches give not that——I'll carry home
The strange experience of some seven hours,
And live upon't hereafter.

CADWAL.
Most brave brother.

CYMBELINE.
We must not lose you so.

PHILARIO.
So please your grace,
I would intreat a word.

CYMBELINE.
Say on, and freely.

PHILARIO.
Then, in the name of all our brotherhood,

I do

CYMBELINE.

I do befeech your majefty to blefs
With your high prefence our poor hermitage;
Which (I am ready to make good the boaft)
Is fit to give a mighty monarch welcome,
If cleanly wholefomenefs, and fimple plenty,
Be worth your appetite; and, fir, the more
I do folicit this, for that I have
Much matter for your ear, which only there
My fpirit groans to utter.——May I hope
This invitation likes your majefty?

CYMBELINE.

Ay, paffing well.——My firs, return you with
A monarch in your train——we long to know
What 'tis you would impart——come thou brave
    fellow!   (*To* Leonatus.)
Some of you lords attend us, and the reft
Abide here in the camp.——Is there clofe guard
Upon the Roman prifoners?

1ft LORD.

        My gracious liege, there is.

CYMBELINE.

'Tis well——Hermit, lead on.

[*Exeunt* Cymbelline, Bellarius, Philario, Palador,
   Cadwal, Leonatus, *and* Lords *at one door,*
   and other Lords *at another.*

The End of the Fourth ACT.

ACT V.

SCENE *The Forest and Cave.*

Enter PALADOR, *and* CADWAL.

PALADOR.

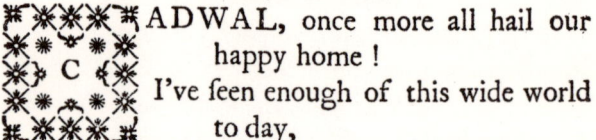

CADWAL, once more all hail our happy home!
I've seen enough of this wide world to day,
To turn my back upon society——
Saving the manly hardiments of war,
There's nought on earth desirable——but come,
Do we our errand, and the cave prepare,
(For therefore were we will'd to speed us first)
For the reception of high majesty.——

CADWAL.
They will o'ertake us soon——

PALADOR.
(*Looking into the cave*)   Stay, come not in——
But that I know this figure, I should think
It were a fairy.

CADWAL.
What's the matter, brother?

PALADOR.
By Jupiter, a spirit!—Gods! one sand
Another doth not more resemble, than
This form the rosy lad who died, and was
Fidele——

CADWAL.
Ev'n the same dead thing alive——

CYMBELINE. 77

PALADOR.
Peace, peace, see more—he eyes us not—forbear—
It is Fidele's ghost——

CADWAL.
    Hist! it comes forward!

Enter IMOGEN *from the cave.*

PALADOR.
Cadwal, stand close — nay shake not — look, it smiles.
What art thou, beauteous vision, that dost take
So sweet a form—thou can'st not mean us harm.
Mischief ne'er travell'd in a shape like that ——
Art thou Fidele? speak—why hast thou left
Thy flow'ry grave? why dost thou haunt our rock?
Or art some spirit in his borrow'd likeness,
That for thy merriment dost wear a semblance,
Deluding us poor mortals? — Gentle, speak. —

IMOGEN.
Give me your hands — I am your living brother,
The true Fidele——

CADWAL.
    Can it be ye Gods!
This is a day of wonders ——

PALADOR.
    I'll no more
Witness the thing I see—art thou alive?
Dear boy, I feel thou art — (*Embracing* Imogen.)

IMOGEN.
    Sirs, I did take
A certain drowsy potion, that fast seiz'd
The present pow'r of life; but in short time

All offices of nature did again
Resume due functions.—Wherefore I took this,
Hereafter ask—and let me now demand,
Where's good Bellarius? where's my uncle? why
Those weapons at your sides? for thus you ne'er
Equip'd for hunting.

PALADOR.

No, my dearest brother,
We've been at better sport in the fair field,
Where honour chases danger—what we've done
Fame shall set down in brass, and shew't to Cæsar;
And then 'twill task arithmetic to count
All the wet cheeks in Rome.

IMOGEN.

How! have your rapiers
Been drawn in battle?

PALADOR.

To victorious purpose —
The king is coming hither ——

IMOGEN.

Hah! the king!
What and who brings him?

PALADOR.

O your worthy uncle,
Unknown, and in disguise; my father too,
And a long lordly train; ere night, the book
Of fate, wide open'd to inspection,
Great secrets shall disclose.—Here comes Philario,
The rest are not far off.—Cadwal, we'll in —
Do you, Fidele, meet him here, and strike
New matter of amazement to his heart.

[*Exeunt* Palador *and* Cadwal *into the cave.*
Enter

CYMBELINE.

Enter PHILARIO.

PHILARIO.
Faireft, and beft of women, pardon me *(kneeling)*
The tortures I have put thy virtue to
In trial, not in malice.—— O forgive me;
For till thy lips have pafs'd remiffion on me,
Mine muft be lock'd in filence.

IMOGEN.
      Rife, Philario!
Thy ftratagem has more complexion in't
Of wifdom, than of guilt —— my honour tried,
I'm ferv'd, and not offended——That fame drug,
Murd'rous awhile to fenfe, I thank'd thee for
With the firft breath I wak'd with—— hence of
  that
Put the remembrance by—My brothers tell me
Of fomething ftrange at hand.——

PHILARIO.
     My gracious lady,
Since laft we parted, the big hours have teem'd
With great, and fad events——pardon me, Gods,
One fiction more.——   *(afide.)*

IMOGEN.
    Haft thou heard aught, Philario,
Of Leonatus? What is in thy mind
That makes thee ftare thus? Wherefore breaks
  that figh
From th' inward of thee? Speak —— where is
  my hufband?

PHILA-

PHILARIO.

Say he were dead—— his villainous intent
Should cure thy prefent forrow.

IMOGEN.

       Thy fuppofing
Confirms his death, and my hereafter woe ——
Thou tell'ft me he was jealous, falfe, and cruel —
Grant he had faults, yet they were faults that others
Haply infus'd into his honeft nature ——
Grant he had faults, yet faults his future life
Might have amended all.——But, oh! this death
Chills mortally, and with the fcythe of winter
Cuts down my fpring of hope——O Leonatus!

PHILARIO.

Nay, lady, mark me — He did leave the world
Without one drop of pity for your fate.
I faw him down in fight, whereto his rage
Had brought him, 'midft the hotteft fumes of war
To make a defp'rate end; and firft explaining
This hermit's garb, (which I to-day put on
To cheat the wary eye of Cymbeline)
Vow'd in the doing his will my heart
Rebell'd againft my hand. " 'Tis well, he cry'd,
" I go to meet the ftrumpet, and confign her
" To other fires than luft." He faid no more,
But to the laft breath'd anger.

IMOGEN.

       If 'tis fo,—
Some dæmon, envious of his peace and mine,
Did witch his fober judgment; nought but magic

CYMBELINE.

In subtle potency of transformation,
Could ruin make of such a noble piece
Of heav'nly workmanship. Gods! what is man
When error outlives honour? Yet, Philario,
I will remember the good thing he was,
Ere fury bent him wrongwards——What he did
Let insolence, that wags his head in scorn
O'er virtue fall'n, proclaim——but never so
Shall his poor wife reproach him——O my lord,
Wise, valiant, gentle, constant, just, and true,
The world did tack to thy all-honour'd name;
Thou wert the mark that Jupiter did point to,
When he prais'd mortal beings.

PHILARIO.
                Noblest princess,
What shall my wonder call thee?—— thy great father
Yet knows not half thy worth—— hither he's coming;
And I will put into his royal pow'r
The now-disposal of our destinies——
Lo, he is here——Be silent, and attend——
Hail to king Cymbeline.——

Enter CYMBELINE, BELLARIUS, LEONATUS,
and Lords.
CYMBELINE.
        We thank you, hermit.——
BELLARIUS.
Good heav'ns! Fidele living!
PHILARIO.
            Hist——a word——
                (Phil. *whispers* Bell.)

CYMBELINE.

In troth, this rock hath a most pleasant site
To tempt a king from home —— O luxury,
How art thou put to shame, if comfort lives
Where lowliness inhabits——our good hosts,
Where are the valiant boys?

PHILARIO.
                    Dread sovereign,
They shall come forth.—Ho! Cadwal! Palador!

Enter CADWAL *and* PALADOR *from the Cave.*

And now, so please your highness, I will ope,
Before you do betake you to repast,
A volume of high marvels to your ear.

CYMBELINE.
Pray you begin.

PHILARIO.
                First know then, mighty sir,
He, that addresses here your royal presence,
No hermit is, but your true slave Philario.——
Nay, start not, sir, but know all criminals,
And then proceed to justice —— here is one
                (pointing to Leonatus.*)*
Has travell'd far to meet your fierce displeasure,
Yet once deserv'd your grace ——

LEONATUS.
                Ay, I am he ——
No beggar, king, but yet a wretch more curst
Than ever fortune spurn'd at.— Know'st me not?
Send for ingenious torturers; command
The art of cruelty to practise on me,
For I do all abhorred things amend
                        By

CYMBELINE. 83

By being worfe than they.— Know'ft me not yet?
The villain that did fteal thy princely daughter;
(Yet that was theft for Gods!) the damned villain
That, in a fit of jealous lunacy,
Murder'd all precious qualities that man
Loves woman for —— that ——

      IMOGEN. *(running, and laying hold of her.)*
           Peace, my lord, hear, hear ——
      LEONATUS.
Shall's have a play of this? thou fcornful page
Come not athwart my grief——   *(ftrikes her.)*
      PHILARIO.
           Hold, Leonatus,
Or thou wilt murder do, who art fo hurt
In a conceit 'tis done — Why gaze you fo?
Didft thou not hear her fpeak? and know'ft thou not
The tune of Imogen?

      CYMBELINE.
           The rock goes round.
      PHILARIO.
Nay, wonder is the gen'ral word to all!
You that ne'er lov'd, look on that virtuous pair—
Mark! how he anchors upon Imogen!
See! how fhe hangs on Leonatus' arm!
While both are mute in fweet extremity
Of trueft love, and joy!

      LEONATUS *(after a paufe.)*
           Joy! who names joy?—
It is a word too cold——What heav'n fhall be
Hereafter, I feel now——Whom had I loft,

But Imogen?———Whom did I hold corrupt,
But Imogen?—Whom did I drive to death,
But Imogen?—Yet Imogen is found—
Yet Imogen is purer than the star
That leads her virgin train to light the morn—
Yet Imogen still lives, and lives to love me!—
—Divide all matter of difcourfe among you——
What can I fay or think but Imogen!

IMOGEN.

How do the gracious Gods hide kindnefs, 'neath
The fable veil of fad appearances?
O Leonatus! had we never parted,
Had I ne'er ftood the mark of thy revenge,
Ne'er had we known what 'tis to meet again,
What 'tis to meet again in life, and love!

(*Embrace.*)

PALADOR.

Why fo, farewel
The boy Fidele! I begin to fear
I fhall hold manhood vile, for fure the graces,
Which fair perfection is compounded of,
Are all bound up in woman! princely Imogen,
Altho' thou art the daughter of a king,
I have ambition in me, that could wifh
To call thee fifter.———

BELLARIUS.

Wond'rous nature ftill! (*afide.*)

PALADOR.

My fword has from their hearts drawn the beft blood
Of thofe you're little bound to———and I'll wear it,
Whilft it is mine, for your protection, lady———

CYMBELINE.

PHILARIO.
I do believ't——enough——now Cymbeline
Wait we your royal sentence——for myself,
That I have cover'd honesty with guile,
In which I had in aim the gen'ral good,
I rather sue for thanks from all, than pardon——
For this my friend, (*points to* Leonatus)—dread
   Sir, your clearest judgment
Has seal'd his virtue sterling; and albeit
In jealous mood he did conceive an act
That tenderness calls terrible, yet think I,
His jealousy had ground more seeming sure,
Than common frenzy treads on——

PALADOR.
      Sir, I know it.

PHILARIO.
Well, by-and-by——for this unparagon'd,
She'as cur'd me of some spleen against her sex;
I've prov'd her (as anon at large you'll hear

IMOGEN.
When we shall make past terrors our disport,)

PHILARIO.
The sweetest lady, and the truest wife,
That ever swore her faith—your sentence, sir,
Which I forestal a kind one.

CYMBELINE.
      Since 'tis thus,
I will not counteract the mighty Gods
In what they have ordained—My children, take
Full pardon in a blessing—heaven's good gifts
Fall on your heads like dew!

LEONATUS.
Thus on our knees—— (*Leonat. and* Imogen *kneel.*)
         Take

Take we with pious thankfulness the bounty.
My Imogen!———
IMOGEN.
My Leonatus!
BOTH.
Oh!——— *(Embracing.)*
PHILARIO.
How glutton-like thou doft devour thy joy,
And can'ft not spare one morsel to a friend!
LEONATUS.
O yes, to thee—for 'tis to thee I owe
The bliss that I am wild with—O believe me,
Scarce went that angry mandate from my hand,
But my repentance fetch'd it back, e'en tho'
I thought my bride-bed ftain'd with violation—
I landed 'midft a herd of vulgar Romans,
In hope to intercept the fell revenge
That freighted thy commiffion, or myfelf
To barter life of future wretchedness
For death of prefent glory—
CYMBELINE.
Well refolv'd—
But still there doth remain behind. Philario,
Long maze to be unravell'd—who are thefe?
This old man and his boys? How join'd you them?
Or knowft thou aught of Cloten, our dear son?
Upon whose widow'd hopes we're bound in honour
To shed some comfort—him we shall endow with
A moiety of this fair realm—
PALADOR.
What him!
Would you make puppets princes? I'm right glad
(Your pardon king) he will not heed your offer—
CYM.

CYMBELINE.

CYMBELINE.
Say'ſt thou bold boy?

PALADOR.
If honeſty is boldneſs,
I am a lion——to be brief, my lord—
Wherefore that frown? I was not born to ſtand
In awe of eye-brows——Your ſon Cloten ranks
'Mongſt thoſe that were your ſubjects——

CYMBELINE.
How is this?
Stripling beware——who trifles with a king
Plays with his peril——

PALADOR.
He is dead—I ſlew him—
Upon the very ſpot thou ſtandſt, I ſlew him——
The fouleſt blood my hand has ſpilt is his——
Monarch, thou knew'ſt him not——

CYMBELINE.
Audacious boy!
Thou haſt condemn'd thyſelf—and ſpight of all
That thou haſt done to-day, doſt from my lips
Pluck a hard ſentence——thou muſt die——

PALADOR.
Hah! hah!
Die, Sir! why then let treaſon be true ſervice,
And loyalty make capital—I'm ſorry
To anger you—but the bare name of Cloten
Untunes my ſpirits; my enraged ſoul
Catches like tinder at it; it doth fret me,
And make me quarrelous and teſty as
Infirmity untended——Good Philario,
Produce thy ſcroll——

PHILA-

PHILARIO.
> Marry, and willingly.
>
> *(Gives* Cloten's *letter.)*
> So please your grace read this. It doth contain
> Matter important to the point. (Cymbeline *reads.*)
> > Good Sirs,
> > Comes it within the compass of belief,
> > Such wisdom and such valour e'er could grow
> > Beneath so poor a roof?——This virtuous hermit
> > Is fit to train up emperors—These youths———
> > But peace——the king

CYMBELINE.
> This letter, sir, whence came it?

PALADOR.
> My lord, Pisanio, with his dying hand
> Lodg'd it in mine——

CYMBELINE.
> It doth appear by this,
> That Cloten villainous connection held
> With the new-beaten Cæsar—I'm abus'd,
> And fool is he that thinks the heart of man
> Hangs at his tongue—loudly this caitif roar'd
> For Britain, and for me; and when he breath'd
> His am'rous plaints, pin'd like a nightingale.—
> This mischief-breeding serpent! Palador,
> We thank thy valour, tho' thy tongue was rude
> In roughness of reply.

PALADOR.
> If I have valour,
> It is my nature, sir, for my harsh language
> I learn'd it 'mongst these rocks.

CYMBELINE.

  We would know more
Of who, and what thou art—Bellarius speak,
Make full discov'ry of yourselves, and fortunes,
And end our present wonders.

BELLARIUS.

    It is meet
Your will should be obey'd—My sons, I must
For my own part unfold much dang'rous truth,
Tho' haply well for you——

PALADOR.

    Your danger's ours.

CADWAL.

And our good your's.

BELLARIUS.

    Most mighty Cymbeline!
Thou hadst a subject that was Edwin call'd.

CYMBELINE.

Edwin! ay, what of him? a banish'd traitor—

BELLARIUS.

Indeed, a banish'd man, but not a traitor;
For I am he—

CYMBELINE.

   The whole world shall not save him!
Lords bear him hence—

BELLARIUS.

Nay, not so hot, great king—First pay me for
The breeding of thy sons—

CYMBELINE.

    Breeding my sons!

BELLARIUS.

I am too blunt, and faucy; here's my knee;
E'er I arife, I will prefer my fons,   *(kneels.)*
Then fpare not the old father. Mighty fir,
Thefe two young gentlemen, that call me father,
Are the true iffue of your royal loins,
And blood of your begetting.

CYMBELINE.

                How! my iffue!

BELLARIUS.

So fure, as you your fire's. Thefe noble princes
(For fuch and fo they are) thefe twenty years
Have I train'd up; fuch arts they have as I
Could put into them—Sir, my breeding was
As your grace knows—Their nurfe Euriphile,
Whom for the theft I wedded, ftole thefe children
Upon my banifhment. The lofs of thefe
The more by you 'twas felt, the more it fhap'd
Unto my end of ftealing them; the vengeance
Of flander'd loyalty—but, royal fir,
Here are your fons again; and I muft lofe
Two of the fweet'ft companions in the world—
Heaven's grace be with them both, for they are
        worthy
To in-lay heav'n with ftars.

CYMBELINE.

              Thou weep'ft, and fpeak'ft—
I loft my children, and if thefe be they
They are a pair of worthies.

BELLARIUS.

                Sir, your patience—

CYMBELINE.

This gentleman whom I call Palador,
Most worthy prince, as your's, is true Guiderius;
This gentleman, my Cadwal, is Arviragus,
Your younger princely son; he, sir, was lapt
In a most curious mantle, wrought by the hand
Of his queen mother, which for more probation
I can with ease produce.

CYMBELINE.

                Guiderius had
Upon his neck a mole, a sanguine star;
It was a mark of wonder.

BELLARIUS.

                 This is he,
Who hath upon him still that nat'ral stamp;
It was wise nature's end in the donation
To be his evidence now.

CYMBELINE.

           'Tis he! 'tis he!
O sure to-day the Gods do mean to strike me
To death with mortal joy— *(Embracing* Palador
      and Cadwal.*)* My sons! my sons!
O Imogen! my child, thou'st found two brothers,
But thou hast lost a kingdom.

IMOGEN.

            No, my lord,
I've got two worlds by this. O my dear brothers,
Do we meet thus? oh! never say hereafter
But I am truest speaker.——You call'd me brother,
When I was but your sister; I, you brothers,
When you were so indeed.

CYMBELINE

PALADOR

       Why e'en let honour
Come, as the Gods forefay it; I'm a prince
But still the British Palador; sweet sister,
The moiety my father meant for Cloten
Is thine, and thy brave lord's, if my request,
The first I make, be granted——thee, Bellarius,
We must at leisure thank; and you, Philario,
We shall set down our friend; dear brother
    Cadwal,
(I can't yet call thee by that other name)
Thou shalt be part'ner of my royalty;
We'll turn our hermitage into a temple,
And yearly smoak it with our sacrifices.

CADWAL.

Agreed! O never was a day like this!

CYMBELINE.

Laud we the Gods!——Bellarius, be our brother.
Sirs, we are much indebted to you all,
And we will shew it in our courtesies——
Come, let us in, and to more joyous feast
Than princes e'er regal'd at——In your stories,
Of which th' abridgement fills us with amazement,
Distinction shall be rich——to-morrow, sirs,
We will to Lud's Town march——Cæsar shall pay
Large ransom for the lives we have in hold,

 And sue to us for terms—ne'er war did cease,
 With fairer prospect of a glorious peace.
        [*Exeunt omnes.*

F I N I S.